Poems on Several Occasions

P O E M S

O N

SEVERAL OCCASIONS:

B Y

Mrs JANE BRERETON.

W I T H

LETTERS to her FRIENDS,

A N D

AN ACCOUNT OF HER LIFE.

LONDON:

Printed by EDW. CAVE at St JOHN'S GATE.

M,DCC,XLIV.

ADVERTISEMENT.

MOST of the following Poems, were written for the Amusement of the Author, and three or four select Friends; and, tho' some of them have been before printed, only a few can be said to be prepared for Publication, as they were to make their Appearance in a feigned Name.

It was necessary to insert several Poems by other Hands, to illustrate the Controversy between *Melissa* and *Fido*, who, tho' he acted a very insincere Part, and had twice the Time to dress up his Answers, as the Reader will find, was very far from obtaining any Advantage.* The Case was thus. The Gentleman who assumed that Name and *Melissa* were near Neighbours, and being conversant in the same Company, the first Epistle which she address'd to *Fidelia*, in *July* 1734 †, she shew'd to him, and ask'd his Advice. Upon which he secretly laid a Scheme to be *Fidelia's* Champion, and accordingly in the *Maga-*

zine

---

* He wrote the lines, p. 231-2, and further to perplex *Melissa*, insisted that they should be signed *E. C.* At last he used up Miss *Manage*, to shift the Scene again; but found his Opponent so formidable a Rival in Parson *Lovemore*, that he was obliged to quit the Field to her superior Wit.

† See this Vol. p. 226.

ADVERTISEMENT.

zine for *August* an Anſwer to *Meliſſa* appeared in the unknown Name of *Fido.* To this
Meliſſa ſoon wrote a Reply, conſulting him
from the firſt rough Draught, as ſhe did on
every other*Occaſion, ſo that before her Pieces reached the Preſs, he was preparing a Return ; and frequently inſerted ſuch Hints as
raiſed in her ſome Surprize, and a Suſpicion
in others, who taxed him with this Piece of
Deceit, but he flatly denied it, and not without the moſt ſhocking Imprecations, endea-
vouring to father theſe Pieces on one or other
of two Gentlemen whom he named. Accordingly *Meliſſa* did not entertain the leaſt Suſpicion of him. But on his unhappy Exit,
(which ſhe mentions with great Concern and
Surprize *p* 310 in the*Magazine* for *May* 1737)
the original Copies in his own Hand-writing
were delivered to her, with other inconteſtable
Proofs —The Controverſy, however, much
enlivened the Entertainment in the Magazines,
and the Editor acknowledges himſelf obliged
to this Lady alſo for ſome other Poems, particularly for the Correction of the *Plaything
charged,* † and of other ſelf-ſufficient Writers.
CON-

* Except when ſhe ſign'd Parſon *Loremore,* which ſomewhat
embaraſſed him

† See *Magazine* for *November* 1736, *p* 678.

CONTENTS.

To

CONTENTS.

By

CONTENTS.

                                To

CONTENTS.

An Account of the Life of Mrs BRERETON.

MR *Thomas Hughes* of *Bryu-Griffith*, near *Mould* in the County of *Flint*, by his Wife Mrs *Anne Jones*, had two Daughters. *Anne*, the eldeſt, died at the Age of Fourteen, to the inexpreſſible Grief of her Parents, her Perſon being extremely beautiful, and having, even in that early Seaſon of Life, diſcover'd an uncommon Share of Underſtanding . But as *Jane* the Younger, who was born in 1685, grew up, (and who is the Subject of theſe Sheets) ſhe ſhew'd her-ſelf no Way inferior to her deceaſed Siſter in the Beauties of her Mind · Her Father ob-ſerv'd, with the utmoſt Pleaſure, the great Ca-pacity with which Nature had endow'd her, and took Care to improve it with all neceſſary In-ſtruction, being himſelf a Perſon of excellent

b   Parts,

Parts, and greatly efteem'd by the Gentlemen of Tafte and Politenefs in the Neighbourhood But he dying when fhe was about fixteen, fhe loft the unfpeakable Advantage of his Converfation and Care, however, her natural Endowments were fo great, that fhe needed little from Art. She foon difcover'd a peculiar Genius for Poetry, which was her chief Amufement; and all her Acquaintance encouraged it by the Delight they took in whatever She compofed. And, before fhe was Twenty, the Perfections of her Mind, the Amiablenefs of her Perfon, and Sprightlinefs of her Temper, render'd her generally admired. On the twenty ninth of *January* 1711, Mrs *Jane Hughes* married Mr *Thomas Brereton*, at that time a Commoner of *Brazen-nofe* College in *Oxford*, only Son of Major *Brereton*, Son and Heir of *William Brereton* of

Efq, an antient Family, in the County Palatine of *Chefter*. The Major's Father being a Roman Catholick had his Son educated at St *Omers*, defigning him for a Prieft; but after he had feen a little into the Bigotry and Superftition of the Church of *Rome*, he return'd Home, determined againft entering into Orders, at which his Father was fo incenfed

cenſed that he diſinherited him. But his Siſter Mrs *Dorothy Brereton*, pitying her Brother's Condition, made him a conſiderable Preſent, tho' ſhe was of the Religion which he renounced, and went afterwards with King *James*'s Court to St *Germains* With her Bounty he bought himſelf a ſmall Poſt in the Army, and behaving with great Bravery under the Duke of *Marlborough*, in ſeveral of his Battles, was raiſed to be a Major. 'Tis hoped it will not be thought a Digreſſion to mention this Particular, ſo much to the Honour of a Convert of the Church of *England*; and it may juſtly be ſaid, that he aim'd at the Reward which is promiſed in the Text, *viz.*
' There is no Man that hath left Father, or
' Mother, or Siſter, or Brother, or Lands,
' for my Sake, or the Goſpel's, but ſhall re-
' ceive an hundred Fold, now in this Time,
' and in the World to come, Life ever-
' laſting.'

When Major *Brereton* died, he left his Son a conſiderable Fortune in Money, but being too young, and in the Management of Guardians, and his Mother marrying Captain *Brown*, there was not that Care taken of his Education that ought to have been: Mr

b 2 *Brereton*

Brereton was fo much a fine Gentleman that he foon ran out moft of his Fortune. He went over for a fhort Time to *Paris*, and, at his Return, the Earl of *Stair*, then Ambaffador there, was pleafed to recommend him, in the ftrongeft Manner, to the Duke of *Marlborough*, as the Son of his old Soldier Major *Brereton*, and his Grace feem'd determined to provide for him, if his ill State of Health had not prevented it. Some Time after this, Mrs *Brereton* was advifed, by all who had any Regard for her, to feparate from her Husband: But tho' all the Reafon in the World pleaded for it, yet fhe exprefs'd great Reluctance at it, efpecially unlefs fhe could have her Children with her; and that being at laft brought about, fhe left *London* about the Year 1721, and retired to her native Country *Wales*, where fhe led a folitary Life, feeing little Company, except fome intimate Friends, Perfons of great Merit, well knowing what a critical Cafe it is to behave without the Cenfure of the World, when feparated from an Husband. Soon after this Mr *Brereton* had a Poft given him by the late Earl of *Sunderland*, belonging to the Cuftoms at *Park-Gate*, near *Chefter*. This

brought

brought him down from *London*. That Nobleman had promifed alſo to advance him on the firſt proper Vacancy ; but he liv'd not to claim it ; for on the ⸺ Day of *February* 1722, he was unfortunately drown'd in adventurouſly croſſing the Water of *Saltney*, when the Tide was coming in His Body was afterwards found, and decently interr'd in *Shotwick* Chapel belonging to *Thomas Brereton*, Eſq, one of the Repreſentatives in Parliament for *Liverpoole*, his intimate Friend and Relation, and in whoſe Service he loſt his Life, for this Gentleman being at that Time concern'd in an Election, with a very powerful Antagoniſt, Mr *Brereton*, out of his great Zeal for his Friend, wrote a Sort of a Libel againſt the Gentleman, and in it he gave himſelf ſuch a Looſe as to come within the Power of the Law ; upon which Mr *Brereton* advis'd him to abſcond to avoid Proſecution (tho' he highly lik'd the Piece which was written by his Inſtigation,) and ſo, by making too much Haſte to get beyond the Knowledge of his Perſuers, ruſh'd into Eternity. He was an unhappy Proof of the Prejudice of an indulgent Education. He uſed to ſay himſelf, that he never in his Life remembered being

contra-

contradicted. His Parts were naturally very good , but entirely neglected. He was very positive and paffionate; but could upon Occasion command himself furprizingly ; so that while he made his Addreffes to Mrs *Hughes*, she took him for a Person of a sweet calm Temper: And his firft Fit of Paffion, after their Marriage, was like a Thunder-clap to her; yet he would fometimes, in a handfome Manner, acknowledge his Fault, and feem fo fenfible, that any, who did not know him too well, would have imagined him fecure againft a Relapfe. He was generous to a Fault, a very indulgent Father, ufed frequently to admire his Wife's Oeconomy, and confefs that his Fortune muft have been fpent long before it was, had it not been for her furprizing Management. He was remarkable for his Skill in Swimming, beyond moft Men, on which he relied too much, at the Time of his Death ; and he was entreated by People on the Shore, not to quit his Horfe, which he would do, and fo perifh'd about the two and thirtieth Year of his Age. He frequently faw his Children, while he was in that Neighbourhood, and had that Satisfaction the very Night before he was loft. So fudden a Death

was

was an inexpreſſible Grief to his Wife, ſhe could hardly ſuppoſt herſelf under the Shock; ſhe fell into violent Faintings, when a Clergyman of great Piety, and a Lady, her intimate Friend, acquainted her with the News, tho' ſhe was perfectly free from any Kind of Fits, till this unhappy Accident.

Soon after this, Mrs *Brereton* remov'd to *Wrexham* in *Denbighſhire*, for the Benefit of her Children's Education, and was herſelf ſoon diſtinguiſh'd by the moſt conſiderable Families in and about that Town. And it muſt be allow'd by all, that that Neighbourhood is remarkable for Politeneſs, Taſte and Hoſpitality. She had the Happineſs and Honour to commence a ſtrict Friendſhip with ſome of the moſt eminent of both Sexes, which continued till the Time of her Death, which happen'd on Thurſday the ſeventh of *Auguſt* 1740 about Nine at Night. Her Diſtemper was the Gravel, which was very afflictive and painful, and laſted about five Weeks, moſt of which Time ſhe was in great Agonies, yet in her Intervals of Eaſe, ſhe was very cheerful, and even the Day ſhe dy'd, ſhe convers'd with an Acquaintance that came to ſee her in a pleaſant

fant Manner She rejoyc'd at every Symptom of approaching Death, and was all Refignation. A fhort Time before fhe expir'd fhe faid, "Now " I'm perfectly eafy and free from Pain, and " will try to fleep," which fhe did, and breath'd her laft in Peace without one Groan. Her Corpfe was handfomely interr'd on the tenth of *Auguft*, in *Wrexham* Church, near the Altar: And on a Pillar adjoyning is a Brafs Plate with the following Infcription; ('till fomething more fuitable to her Memory can be erected) " Here Lies the Body of *Jane* " *Brereton*, Widow of *Thomas Brereton*, " Gent. who departed this Life, *Auguft* the " 7th, 1740. Aged 55.

Her Perfon was of a middle Stature, well fhaped and eafy, her Complexion inclining to Brown; her Hair a dark Brown, a good Forehead, fire arch'd Eye-brows, fmall grey Eyes, a remarkable handfome Nofe, an a- greeable Mouth, and a fine Set of Teeth: Her Face was well turn'd, an engaging Sweetnefs was diffufed over her Coun- tenance. She had four Children, *Tho- mas* and *John*, who died Infants, and lie bu- ried at *London*, and two Daughters, *Lucy* and *Charlotte*, both Living, the Eldeft with

her

her Uncle in *Cork,* and the other at *Stratford,* in *Essex.*

She was the most affectionate and dutiful Wife; and always behav'd with good Humour, Patience and Submission. This might afford a large Field for displaying her Virtues · But as it can't be done, without casting a Cloud on Mr *Brereton,* those who stand in the same Relation to both, chuse to have it omitted, believing there is enough to give Lustre to her Character, without making another's a Foil to it. She was the most indulgent tender Parent, chusing to govern her Children more by Love than Fear, and was particularly anxious about her Daughters Education, and instilling into their Minds Religion and Virtue ; and would often with Tears say to them, ' My Dear Girls, you " don't know what Snares and Temptations " there are for young Women, in this wick- " ed, designing World, to draw your Hearts " from God· But if you'll in every Thing " rely on his Providence, and make him the " sole Object of your Love, he will guard " you from them all ; and you'll find his " Promise accomplish'd of being a Father to " the Fatherless." She was extremely devout and obfervant of all religious Duties, was regular in her own Devotions, and conftantly twice a Day call'd her little Family together to Prayers When fitting only with her Children, fhe frequently lifted up her Heart to God in pious Ejaculations, ever with the greateft Gratitude acknowledging his Care of her and hers; and acquiefcing with an entire fubmiffion to his Difpenfations. Tho' fhe liked Wit, fhe could never bear any Thing that feem'd to her to be fcurrilous, and fome Things that fhe wrote, at the Entreaty of her Friends, that were a little Satirical, afterwards gave her great Uneafinefs. She was a true Member of the Church of *England*; but had great Charity for all thofe of different Perfuafions. She had a ftedfaft Affection and Loyalty for the prefent Royal Family, as may be feen in her Works. But that did not prevent her being on good Terms of Friendfhip with fome Ladies of Diftinction, tho' of an oppofite Opinion; for fhe had the moft exalted Notions of Friendfhip, and never in the fmalleft Article fwerv'd from its Rules. She was an excellent Miftrefs ufing her Servants like her Children, and thought the Souls of her Servants were Part of her Care,

Care, as well as their Bodies; and would therefore hear them herself read a Chapter out of some of the Gospels, and see that they understood it, and show'd an Inclination to follow those sacred Rules. Her Care of the Poor was ever impress'd on her Mind· She allotted on Friday an Allowance to be given them at her own Door As it was the Day on which the Saviour of Mankind suffer'd, she thought it most proper to make some Acknowledgement to his poor Members, besides such occasional Charities as her small Income would afford.

She made it her Business to find out distress'd Objects, and recommend them to her Acquaintance; and used to go herself, and see them in their Houses, and examine into their Circumstances, that she might give to each, in proportion to their Wants; and by this Search frequently found out some very miserable Objects, who either from Age, or very great Infirmities, could not make their Condition known. She was extremely modest and diffident of herself, and spoke but little, when with much Company. She liked Music, and sung agreeably, and sometimes play'd at Cards, tho' but a bad Play-

er,

er ; as she used to say, they could never engage her Thoughts enough to mind her Game,
and therefore she never made a Party but to o-
blige others. She approv'd much of a well written Play, chiefly Tragedies, and believ'd that
well chosen Ones very much improved the
Minds of young Persons, and gave them many just and delicate Sentiments, but could not
bear Romances, nor any Thing inclining that
way. She was very nice in the Choice of her
Poetry, tho' when a bad Poem came thro'
her Hands, she pass'd no Reflections on the
Author, and would only make some innocent
Joke of it. She would indeed sometimes say,
she pitied the Author that knew not how to
apply his Talent to greater Profit. Her
Poetical Name of *Melissa* was given her
by a Gentleman of her Acquaintance, from
the Latin Word *Mell*, as bearing some
Allusion to the Sweetness of her Numbers.
Writing was her darling Entertainment, and
was to her a Relaxation from her Cares; tho'
she would not consent to have her Works
published by Subscription, when proposed by
a Gentleman, in a very pressing Manner. She
approv'd of a particular Sanctity of Behaviour on Sunday, and always commended the

Dissenters

Diffenters for training up their Children by
that Rule; and for not allowing them what
fome call innocent Sport, for their Health,
on that Day; which fhe thought fhould be
employ'd in a more ferious Manner, even by
Children, for as *Solomon* tells us, " Train up
" a Child in the Way which he fhould go,
" *&c.*" Tho' fhe was of a very cheerful Temper, and fhew'd a great deal of Life and Fire,
fhe thought too much Aufterity, even in the
moft important Subjects, only gave frightful
Ideas of Religion, and terrified, inftead of
charming, the gayer Part of the World.

She had only one Brother *Thomas*, who,
being a little unlucky at his firft fetting out
in Life, fold his Eftate of *Bryn-Griffith*, and
went to *Ireland*, where, applying to the Bufinefs of a Brewer, he had fuch Succefs as to
raife a plentiful Fortune, and is now one of
the moft confiderable Men in the City of *Cork.*
He was very defirous of his Sifter's fpending
with him, the latter Part of her Life, but fhe
thought her Situation fo agreeable at
Wrexham, that fhe excufed herfelf, tho' it
would have been advantageous to her : For
fhe was quite free from all mercenary Views.
Art was a Stranger to her, and Deceit fhe ab-
horr'd,

horr'd, with every Thing in Speech, or Behaviour, that wanted true Delicacy. Her Memory will ever be rever'd by all who knew her, and when her youngest Daughter was in *Wales*, about two Years after her Death, some Ladies of the first Rank both in Fortune, and Understanding, could not mention her Name without Floods of Tears, particularly those Ladies to whom the Verses, and Ballad are addrefs'd in her Poems (Page 37 and 39) and in the fincereft Manner regretted the Lofs (as they exprefs'd themfelves) of fo wife, and entertaining a Friend ; and her Daughter as fhe went thro' the Streets, had Bleffings pour'd upon her by the Poor whom her Mother had frequently reliev'd, not only with her own Mite, but by making Application for them to Perfons of Fortune, and Generofity, fo that fhe was feveral Times oblig'd to turn into a Friend's Houfe, or take fome by-way, to avoid the public Acknowledgement of thefe poor People ; efpecially as it excited fo many mix'd Senfations of Pain and Pleafure in her Soul, that fhe was often ready to fink under the Oppreffion.—She had a very low Opinion of herfelf, and always confefs'd the great Honour that was done her by the Acquaintance

quaintance of so many Persons of diftinguifh'd Senfe; and feldom receiv'd a Letter from a young Lady of eminent Merit and Learning, an Ornament to her Sex, and who corresponded with her towards the Clofe of her Life, but she acknowledged her Surprize, how one so learn'd and univerfally admired, could be the leaft pleas'd with her artlefs unpolifh'd Epiftles (as she called them) and frequently exprefs'd her obligations to that Lady for every Line she favour'd her with.

It only can be added, that she was Amiable in every Character of Life, as the modeft Maid, the chafte and prudent Wife, the tender and fond Parent, the decent Widow, the fincere and wife Friend, the indulgent Miftrefs, and the good, pious and exemplary Chriftian.

✵✵✵✵✵✵✵✵✵✵ ✵✵✵✵✵✵✵✵✵✵✵✵✵✵ ✵✵✵✵✵✵✵✵✵✵

As nothing better expresses the true Charact-
ers of Persons, than their Epistolary Cor-
respondence with their Friends, in which
the Mind opens itself without Reserve, the
Editor has thought proper to insert a few
of Mrs Brereton's Letters, which may
serve to shew, at once, her Sincerity, easy
Elegance of Expression, and the affectionate
Warmth of her Friendship.

✵✵✵✵✵✵✵✵✵✵✵✵✵✵ ✵✵✵✵✵. ✵✵✵✵✵ ✵✵✵✵✵✵✵✵✵✵✵✵✵

LETTER I.

To Mrs M-----D-----N, 1726.

MADAM,

I Think myself highly oblig'd to you,
for favouring me with Mr *Law*'s and
Mr *Bedford*'s Discourses, and think it
my Duty to acquaint you with the result of
my Reading : You will believe that what I
offer is with the greatest Submission and De-
ference to your superior Judgment. I have
seen nothing that has been written against either; so that all I have to plead in defence of
my Opinion, are merely such Reflections as

occurr'd

occurr'd to me in Reading. I think after confidering their Reafons, as far as a perplex'd Head, and weak Capacity, would permit, I can't fubfcribe to their Sentiments; but if hereafter their Arguments fhould appear to me to have greater Weight, I fhall be willing to be convinc'd, and to confefs my Error.

That our Plays in general are full of Impiety is undeniable, but it does not neceffarily follow that it is effential to Plays to be fo, and a Remedy might fure be found without fuppreffing them. The Poets have often complain'd that it was in compliance with the corrupt Tafte of the Audience that they wrote fuch Stuff, and the Criticks affirm that a juft Reprefentation of Life muft have mix'd Characters in it. However, the Poet, I think, is very faulty, when he reprefents Vice in an alluring Manner, or endeavours to make Virtue ridiculous. To fee Villany triumphant, and Truth or Innocence opprefs'd, leaves but an ill Impreffion on the Minds of the Audience. Therefore, if there were lefs regard paid to critical Rules, and more to Modefty, and poetical Juftice, our modern Plays would not be fo exceptionable as they are. I fhould

d   rejoyce

rejoyce to fee our Theatre fo reform'd and
regulated, and fhould then look on Dramatic
Entertainments as the moft rational of all Diverfions. There is no Amufement whatever,
but may be abus'd and corrupted; one may
grow impatient, and avaritious at any Game
that is innocent enough in itfelf, Dancing is
thought to be a healthful Exercife, and a
very inoffenfive Recreation; and yet fome
have been of Opinion that it is productive
of ill Effects. The primitive Chriftians, I
know, condemn'd all Stage Plays, and I would
gladly be inform'd, if they allow'd of any
Diverfions at all. The Church was then in
its Infancy, and apprehenfive of being feduc'd by the Sports and Cuftoms of the Hea-
thens. All the Dramatic Performances, Greek
and Latin, were full of the Heathen Mytho-
logy and Polytheifm, their Rites and Sacri-
fices; which were juftly an Abomination to
the Jews, and Chriftians. Some of the Fathers were converted from Paganifm, and it
feem'd proper they fhould fhew the Sincerity
of their Converfion by expreffing their Detef-
tation of thofe Manners and Cuftoms which
they had but lately relinquifh'd. Befides, the
primitive Church for the moft Part was under

                   Perfecution;

Perſecution; and if God, for the Puniſhment
of this Nation, ſhould permit the ſame Spirit
to rage among us; and that we were appa-
rently in the ſame Danger, as they were in;
doubtleſs there are Numbers who now do not
appear over zealous in the Cauſe of Religion;
who in a Time of Perſecution would not indulge themſelves in any Sports ; and conſe_
quently would deny themſelves the Diverſion
of the moſt innocent Play that ever was
penn'd. But the Wiſe Man ſays, " there is
" a Time for all Things." Both the Time
and the Nature of Things made it neceſſary
for the Fathers to declare and act as they did.
I am miſtaken, if they allow'd of any Diver-
ſions ; but wean'd themſelves from the
World, and *dy'd daily*, in expectation of that
Death, which they were continually appre-
ſive of ſuffering from the Spirit of Perſecution, which rarely ſlept in thoſe Days. For
the ſame Reaſon it was that they ſo frequently receiv'd the Sacrament ; which in After-a-
ges was not judg'd abſolutely neceſſary to be
ſo often repeated.

It may be alleg'd, that obſcene Ideas, and
profane Expreſſions, ought to be as abomina-
ble to every chaſte and religious Ear, as the

Heathen Theology, Rites, &c. were to the Fathers; this is evident Truth. But, if Perfons of Diftinction would once difcountenance fuch Performances by their abfence, it would probably reform our Stage more than any Thing that can be written againft it. Such a Conduct would encourage thofe who could write with Purity and Delicacy; and oblige others to prune the pernicious Witticifms, which render their (otherwife entertaining) Plays very offenfive. I, would, at leaft, fet Plays upon a level with Dancing, Back-Gamon, or a Game at Cards, &c. tho' in my own Opinion, I prefer a well-wrought Play to them all, but would plead for it only as an Amufement. For, with Regard to improving our Morals, I feek not that in a Play; we are abundantly fupply'd with neceffary Inftructions for that Purpofe, in the Works of learned and religious Men; and enjoy the ineftimable Bleffing of having a free Recourfe to the Fountain of eternal Truth. But if under the Chriftian Difpenfation, we are allow'd any Diverfions, I can't conceive why Plays are not as innocent as any other; they might, if well regulated, be made preferable to all. I do not apprehend that Mr *Law* has fully

demonftrated

demonſtrated *the abſolute Unlawfulneſs of* *Stage Entertainments* ; nor can he do it, unleſs he firſt prove, that it is abſolutely Unlawful to relate the Actions, repreſent the Perſon, or repeat the Words of another. There is, I think, a Difference between abſolutely unlawful, and ſimply unlawful ; ſo, I ſuppoſe, he means (tho' he has not prov'd it) that it is unlawful to repeat even the moſt noble Sentiments and elevated Thoughts. If he can demonſtrate that, it will neceſſarily follow, that it is unlawful to relate a Story, or repeat a Speech out of *Plutarch, Clarendon, &c.* And to me 'tis evident, that ſuch Inferences would be deducible from that Hypotheſis, as would extend further than the Author himſelf ever intended. I look on Mr *Bedford* and Mr *Law,* as religious and well diſpos'd Men, but even ſuch may be carry'd away by their Prejudices. If their Arguments have not convinc'd me, I aſſure you, Madam, 'tis wholly the fault of my Underſtanding, which can't comprehend any great force in their Way of Reaſoning ; ſo that all the Benefit I have receiv'd by them, is confirming me in what has long been my Opinion —" That our Stage ought to be reform'd." Thus, Madam,

I have

LETTER I.

I have prefum'd in an unmethodical manner to write my Thoughts on thefe Authors, and offer my Reafons why I can't fubmit to their Arguments. I am not fo Vain as to fuppofe my Opinion is of any Confequence but to myfelf; but, when it is ask'd, I think it my Duty to anfwer with Truth and Integrity; tho' I fhould hardly venture to write my Notions to any, but fuch whofe Benevolence and Candour are as extenfive as their Under-ftanding and Knowledge. You, Madam, I am perfuaded, are of that happy Number; and therefore I defpair not of your excufing this Rhapfody from, &c.

LETTER II.

To Mrs M-----D-----N.

LETEER II

MADAM,

I Have kept Mr *Law* very long, but was loth to part with him till I had exa-min'd him thoroughly. I thought no-thing could be added to his former Treatife; and, indeed, if the Performance is equal to the Title, nothing ought to be added to

                             Chriftian

Chriſtian Perfection: But I think he is more rigid in this Piece, than in his former.

If all Women of Fortune were *Mirandas,* how many Families that are now ſupported by Trade, would be reduc'd to Want and Beggary? For there need be but few Hands, and fewer Materials employ'd, to dreſs up a Lady, to make no better an appearance, than a *neat and clean Country Girl.* 'Tis true, by this frugality in Dreſs the Lady may be enabled to beſtow more in Alms; but would not ſuch a Procedure increaſe the Number of the Poor? And is it not a greater Charity to prevent People from falling into Diſtreſs, than to relieve them when they are in it? Doubtleſs it is: For while they are in a Way of Buſineſs, they may by their Induſtry maintain themſelves, and contribute ſomething towards the Relief of the Neceſſitous. Whereas, if they are not employ'd, they muſt come in for a Share in what might have been wholly appropriated for the comfortable Support of the aged, helpleſs and infirm. I am not skill'd in drawing Characters, but I could point to a living Example of this religious Turn of Mind, the ſame Benevolent and Alms-giving Diſpoſition, and the ſame

Chriſtian

Christian Frame of Spirit as he describes, and of a more extensive Charity than that of *Miranda*'s. What the excellent *Maria* expends in decently maintaining that Rank and Station in which Providence has plac'd her, is in its Effects the highest Charity; as it helps to cloath, and feed Numbers of her Fellow-Creatures. If there were any Sin in wearing fine Garments, we may be certain the meek and humble Patriarch would not have bestow'd such on his Son *Joseph*, nor the holy Prophet allow'd the Use of such to his Daughter *Thamar*. In the 5th Paragraph of his last Chapter the Author owns plainly, " that Voluntary Poverty, *&c.* and such o-" ther *Restraints* of *lawful* Things, are not " necessary to Christian Perfection, but are " much to be commended in those, who " chuse them as Helps, *&c.*" But, if they are not necessary to Christian Perfection, I think the recommending of them is very unnecessary; unless the Author would advance Works of Supererogation. Tho' some exalted Spirits, who can renounce the pleasurable Enjoyments of Life, may relish his rigid Doctrine, it is to be fear'd, it may prove to others a Stumbling Block. I really have a Veneration for

Mr

Mr *Law*, as I believe him to be a very pi- ous Man; and tho' I take the freedom with you, Madam, to own that I differ from him in my Judgment of several Things, yet I affure you, I fhall never repent of my reading him. Several of his Reflections, *Paternus*'s Inftructions to his Son, and *Eufebia*'s to her Daughters, in the main, pleafe me very much, I wifh I may keep them in my Memory. I defign'd only a few Lines to thank you, good Madam, for *Law* and *Sturmy*, but I have been led away by the Subject beyond, I fear, the Bounds of your Patience, and you will perhaps wifh Pen and Ink had been out of my Reach. But, dear Madam, (allow me the Freedom of that affectionate Epithet, for dear you are to all that know you, and more fo, to me than I can ever exprefs) don't be angry at my long Scribble, 'tis not that I am fond of Writing, but my Mind fuffers fo much on the Account of my Family, that I am glad now and then to give it a little Relaxation. Be pleas'd to accept of my grateful Thanks for your laft Favour to *Charly*, and with your ufual Goodnefs to pardon the Prolixity of

April 30*th*, 1729.

c   LETTER

✿✿✿✿✿✿✿✿✿✿✿✿✿✿✿✿✿✿✿✿✿✿✿✿✿✿

LETTER III.

To Miſs * * * *, *in anſwer to*
hers of November 1.

Mᴀᴅᴀᴍ,

THE Eſteem which the well diſpos'd
and learned Miſs ᴛ*ᵀ** expreſſes
for me, gives me a high Satisfaction.
But as every Pleaſure has its Alloy, ſo my
own Diffidence will not ſuffer me to think
myſelf entitled to ſo much Merit, as you are
pleas'd to complement me with. Our favourite Ideas are ſometimes ſo high wrought,
that when we ſee the Perſons or Things, that
firſt occaſion'd them, we ſeldom find them
reach that Perfection, which our indulgent
Imagination had adorn'd them with.—Shall
I then revoke the Wiſh in my laſt · For,
ſhou'd we happen to meet, I muſt inevitably
ſink in your Opinion, and what a Diſappoint-
ment muſt that be to you, after the high I-
dea you had conceiv'd in my Favour ! And
what a Mortification would it be to me, to
find

find myfelf incapable of maintaining an E-
fteem that did me fo much Honour ' Well ;
Whatever is, is right.   And as, at this Dif-
tance, I have no room to hope for the Pleafure of your Perfonal Converfation ; fo on
the other Hand, fince 'tis not likely that we
fhall meet, I have no ground to fear, that
mine fhould leffen me in your Opinion ———
The Word *Opinion*, (which I now find, I
am fo fond of, as to ufe it more than once in
a few Lines) brings to my Mind the Title of an *Italian* Book, which the celebrated Mr *Pafcal* mentions.—" Opinion the
" Queen of the Univerfe."—Certainly, her
Power is more extenfive, and fometimes more
conducive to our Happinefs, than that of
Knowledge.   And, I muft confefs, 'tis to her
good Influence alone, that I am oblig'd for
the Pleafure of your Correfpondence.   I
have lately read in the Works of the Learned, with much Satisfaction, fome Extracts
from feveral excellent Difcourfes by a Reverend of your Name.   Your Name, and your
Practice turn'd my Thoughts on you , and I
could not forbear taking a particular Notice
of the firft Branch of his Definition of the
Precept of doing Good.   " To do Good,

e 2   ' fays

" fays that judicious Preacher, is to endea-
" vour after the Comfort and Pleafure of O-
" thers." 'And how much you, Madam,
are dispos'd to that beneficent Duty, is demonftrated by the pious Reflections, and
humane Tendernefs, exprefs'd in your obliging
Letters · By which you have engaged me
to be, very fincerely,

      Your affectionate humble Servant.
Dec. 5, 1738.   J. B.

LETTER IV.

To Mifs ****, *in anfwer to
hers of* March 22, 1739.

MADAM,

I Should not wonder if you, by this Time,
had heartily repented of commencing
an Epiftolary Acquaintance with fo
ftupid a Correfpondent. I told Mr *Cave* in
my laft that I was too dull to attempt writing to you, I am under the Influence of the
fame Heavinefs ftill ; but having no hopes of

                            over-

overcoming it, I chufe rather to have my Letter thought dull, than my Silence rude. What I wrote on the Sermons, was meant as a grateful Teftimonial of the edifying Entertainment they had afforded me ; and I deferve no Thanks, for acknowledging a Benefit.

I am glad to find myfelf in the fame way of thinking with you. The more I am pleas'd with an Author, the more defirous I am that others fhould partake of the Pleafure. I believe moft Readers are of this communicative Temper ; and that few defire to monopolize a Satisfaction of this Kind. The Clafs of Readers are the very Reverfe of the Tribe of Lovers. They are always delighted when they have Partners in their Pleafures; and even embrace all opportunities to folicit others to be their Rivals! This has often been my Cafe; and feems now to be yours, with regard to Mrs *Rowe*'s Works. She had a fine Genius; and no Attachments in this World, to prevent her indulging, and improving it. Her Stile is flowing, and perfectly Poetical ; her Defcriptions are exceeding lively · And I have fometimes thought that her Profe abounds with more ftriking

Images

Images than her Vêrfe. There is in the firft
Collection fhe publifh'd, a very good Para-
phrafe on the third Chapter of *Habakkuk*,
in a Pindaric Ode, or rather an irregular
Ode . For I believe *Pindar*'s Odes were as
exact, and regular, as any Species of Poetry.
I have feen her Verfes on her Husband's
Death, her Letters, and her *Jofeph*; and
alfo her devout Exercifes, lately publifh'd by
Dr*Watts*, which indeed exprefs a high Strain
of Devotion. I acknowledge the Force of
her Genius, and the Goodnefs of her Inten-
tion. But will dear Mifs **** forgive me,
if I fhould fay of fome of Mrs *Rowe*'s Letters, particularly thofe from the Dead, what
a Reverend Dignitary faid the other Day of
the Spectators ?—" That they were moral,
" and entertaining, but he believ'd they ne-
" ver made one Convert to Religion" I
could not fubmit to his Judgment, nor do
I expect you to agree with mine, when I
confefs, that in my Opinion, there breathes
too much of the Air of Enthufiafm in her
Letters. The Defign of the Letters from
the Dead, (fhe fays in the Preface) is to imprefs a Notion of the Soul's Immortality.
We will fuppofe then, that a Perfon who
doubts

doubts of that important Article, reads thofe Letters, and receives the defired Impreffion. May not the Mind, juft enlightened, be dazled with the Splendor of Defcriptions ? and the Soul pant for ————" the delectable " Vales and flowery Lawns, the Myrtle " Shades and rofy Bowers, the bright Caf- " cades and cryftal Rivulets of Paradife ? May not the Head be turned with thefe waking Dreams, and the Heart never wifh for a Felicity beyond a Pagan Elizium ? I have the greateft Opinion of her Underftanding, and the higheft Veneration for her Piety; and yet I fear her fine Defcriptions will be of no Service to Religion. She had a good deal of Enthufiafm, and the Warmth of that, tranfported her Imagination into the invifible World, and infpired her to point out thofe Wonders which no Eye has feen, and no Tongue repeated. I muft own, that I have no great Relifh for any Difplay of the Happinefs of Immortality, but what is warranted by Scripture.

Mrs *Rowe's* Sentiments are noble, and her Language is beautiful. Had Mr *Pope's* Effay on Man appeared before her Letters, I

doubt

doubt not, but many Readers would have imagined that she imitated this Couplet of his—

    " Warms in the Sun, refreshes in the
         Breeze,
    " Glows in the Stars, and blossoms in the
         Trees,

                     1st Ep. 1. 263.

But long before he published his Essay, she
had expressed herself, in the following beautiful Manner.—" He chears me in the Glory
" of the Sun, refreshes me in the fragrant
" Breeze, is Beauty in the Flowers of the
" Field, and Harmony in the Nightingale's
" Voice."

But who dares say, that the great Poet copy'd Mrs *Rowe* ?

I imagined from what you said in yours of
Mrs *Rowe*, that you expected me to give my
Opinion of her. I have done it, in an unre-
served, and I may add, in a very incorrect
manner, tho' I hope my Sincerity in it will
not lessen your Esteem for,   Madam,

         Your affectionate Friend, and oblig'd
                   humble Servant.
     April 24,
     1739   J. B.

                       LETTER

LETTER V.

To Miss * * * *,

In answer to hers of December 2, 1739.

I Grant you, Madam, that Pride is an in-
sinuating and predominant Passion; but
that there is the least Appearance, or
Symptom of it, in your Letter, is what I can
by no means admit. Nothing can be more
just than your Sentiments of that Passion,
and nothing less so, than your Application of
it to yourself. There is certainly a Pleasure
in the giving, or receiving a just disinterested
Approbation, but I cannot believe, that a
Pleasure of this Nature is either a Cause, or
a Consequence of Pride: On the contrary,
I apprehend it to be, the pure Joy, and
Satisfaction, which a benevolent Mind receives
from whatever is Praise-worthy.

It must be confess'd that Pride is a sort of
a *Proteus*; it can vary its Form, to gratify

f   its

its own Vanity, or to elude Difcovery It
is fometimes imperceptible, where it bears
the greateft Sway , and, on the other Hand,
it is often fufpected to be where it really is
not. As, for Inftance, in the Article of
Drefs. A fafhionable Garb, put on in a
genteel Manner, is, in the Opinion of fome
rigid People, an infallible Indication of
Pride. But if, as fome have thought, (and
if my Memory deceives me not, Mr *Ray*
fays) the improving and beautifying the
Earth, with Plantations, Gardens, &c. ought
to be confidered as a religious Duty , why is
it not as laudable in the Chief of the Creation
to adorn themfelves with all the Elegance of
Drefs, fuitable to their Age and Condition,
and conformable to the Mode of the Country
they live in ?

Some Divines have taught, that the Confideration of the richeft Garments being chiefly
made of the Bowels of an ugly Worm, fhould
humble the Wearer —True;—But may not
this be an Argument for wearing that, which
affords an humbling Confideration?

Mr *Law*, in his Character of *Miranda* (in
his *Call to a devout and holy Life)* fays, fhe
dreffes meanly, that fhe may be able to fup-
port

port indigent Families. There are Calamities and Circumſtances, which ought to be particularly conſidered. But, in the general, is there not greater Charity in employing the Induſtrious, and, conſequently, preventing them from being reduc'd to Poverty, than in relieving them when they are ſo? There may be, I am perſuaded, as much Pride in the Contempt of Dreſs, as in too great a Fondneſs of it. Who doubts, but that *Diogenes* was prouder in his Tub than *Plato* on his Carpet? The Remark which that polite Philoſopher made on ſeeing the *Cynic* up to the Chin in Water was certainly very juſt.—But where am I rambling?—I know not how far I might have expatiated on this Topic, which you threw in my Way, had not the ſhocking Thought of the Situation, the mad *Cynic* was in, joyn'd with the ſevere Coldneſs of the Weather, ſet me a ſhuddering, tho' by a good Fire, and, happily for you, put a ſtop to my Speculations.

I ſhould be glad to know the Name of the Ship, which your Friend goes in, that I may rejoyce with you, tho' at the Diſtance of two hundred Miles, when I read in the News,

that

that fhe is fafely arriv'd in the *Downs,* with a rich Prize.

I have made a long Paper-Vifit , but as I have not been able to fay any thing enter-taining, I think the moft obliging Thing I can do, is to take my Leave: So fhall only ftay to affure you, that I am,

Dear Madam !

Jan. 18, 1740.   *Yours,* &c.

J. B.

SUBSCRIBERS

T O

Mrs *Brereton's* Poems.

PATRICK Agnew of Teragle, Efq, 4to
    Mr David Agnew of Wigton **4to**
Mrs Aubrey of Chefter 4to
Mifs Allington 8vo
Right Hon. Vifcountefs Bulkely 4to
Mrs Bennet, two Books 4to
Thomas Brereton, Efq, two Books 4to
Mrs Brereton of Borras 4to
Mrs Bowman 4to
Rev. Mr Boyde of Wigton 8vo
Rev Mr Burnet 8vo
Rev. Mr Birch 8vo
Right Hon. Lady Betty Cotton 4to
      Ditto 8vo
Lady Chapman 4to
Captain Chefter 4to
Mifs Carter 4to
Dr Campbell of Wigton 8vo
John Campbell of Aries, Efq, 8vo
John Cleland, Efq; 8vo
Mifs Cuxon 8vo
Mrs Davies of the Mount 4to
      Ditto 8vo

Robert

SUBSCRIBERS.

Robert Davies of Lanerch, Efq; 4to
Mrs Drelincourt 4to
Right Hon. the Earl of Eglinton 4to
Mrs Eyles 4to
Thomas Eyton of Leefwood, Efq, 8vo
Mrs Jane Edwards of Ruthin 8vo
Mr Robert Fowlis of Glafgow 8vo
The moft Honourable the Marchionefs of
 Grey 4to
The Right Hon. Lady Mary Grey 4to
The Right Hon. the Earl of Galloway 4to
The Right Hon. the Lord Garlies 4to
The Right Hon. the Lady Garlies 4to
John Griffiths of Garn, Efq, 4to
Her Grace the Dutchefs of Hamilton 2
 Books 4to
Patrick Heron of Kirochtree, Efq, 4to
Rev. Mr Holland of Marchwiel 4to
Mrs Hall of Chefter 4to
Mr Holford of Flint 4to
Mr Thomas Hughes of Cork 4to
Mr John Hughes of Cork 4to
Mr Hayman of Wrexham 8vo
Mr Clement Hart, London-wall 8vo
Rev. Mr Lewis Jones of Ruthin 8vo
Rev Mr Richard Jones of Wrexham 8vo
John Robinfon Lytton, Efq; 4to
Rev. Mr Lawry, Prebendary of Rochefter 4to
Lady Longueville 4to
Edward Lloyd of Tuthyn, Efq, 4to
Mrs Lloyd of Chancery Lane 4to
Capt. Levett, of Warwick Street 4to
Foulk Lloyd of Brynliarth, Efq; 8vo

Mr

SUBSCRIBERS.

Mr Hercules Lindefay of Glafcow 8vo
Mrs Jane Lewis of Ruthin 8vo
Rt Hon. the Countefs of Murray 4to
Right Hon. Lady Euphemia Murray 4to
Hon. Alex. Murray of Broughton, Efq; 4to
James Murray, Efq, 8vo
Mrs Myddelton of Croesnewydd, 2 Books 4to
Mrs Manwaring of Chefter 4to
Mifs Moftyn of Kilkin 4to
Mifs Elizabeth Moftyn 4to
Mifs Margaret Moftyn 4to
John M'dogel of Logan, Efq; 4to
Alex. Maxwell, Efq, 4to
William Maxwell of Ardwell, Efq, 8vo
Mr David Maxwell 4to
Capt. James M'guffog 4tô
Rev. Mr John Millar Clavy 8vo
Mr John Meredith of Wrexham 8vo
John Nelfon, Efq; 4to
The Right Hon. the Lady Vifcountefs Prim-
    rofe 4to
Mr Robert Patterfon of Edinburgh 4to
Mrs Parry of Plas-y-rhall, two Books 8vo
Rev. Dr Powell, Dean of St Afaph 4to
The Right Hon. Countefs of Seaforth 4to
The Right Hon. Lady Anne Stewart 4to
The Hon. Mifs Stewart 4to
The Hon. Mifs Sufanna Stewart 4to
The Hon. Mifs Margaret Stewart 4to
The Hon. Mifs Euphemia Stewart 4to
The Hon. Brigadier John Stewart 4to
The Hon. Col James Stewart 4to
The Hon. Capt. William Stewart 4to
Mrs Stewart of Caftle Stewart 4to

                                    Capt.

SUBSCRIBERS.

Capt. John Stewart of Phifgil 4to
George Shakerly, Efq; 4to
Mr Griffith Speed of Wrexham 4to
William Sinclair of Rofline, Efq; 4to
Rev. Mr Smith of Chefter 8vo
Mr John Smith of Wigton 8vo
Dr James Stonehoufe of Northampton 8vo
Edward Thellwall, Efq; 4to
Mifs Thellwall 8vo
John Travers, Efq; 4to
Mrs Travers of London 4to
Mifs Travers 4to
Mr William Travers, jun. 4to
Mr Walter Thomas of Chefter 8vo
Mrs Underdown of Deal 8vo
Mr Vafton of Leominfter 8vo
Lady Wilhams 4to
   Ditto 8vo
Lady Williams Wynne 4to
Mrs Williams of Bryn-y-junon 4to
Mrs Whitmore of Thurftafton, 2 Books 4to
Mifs Wynne of Plas-new-ydd, 3 Books 4to
   Ditto, three Books 8vo
Matthew Wymondefold, Efq, 2 Books 4to
John Broughton Whitehall of Broughton,
  Efq, 4to
Kuffin Williams, Efq; 4to
Rev. Mr Williams, Rector of Hawardin 4to
Mrs Dorothy Wynne of Rhofe 8vo
Pierce Wynne of Duffrynated, Efq, 8vo
Mr Whitfield of Chefter 8vo
The Hon Philip Yorke, Efq; 4to
The Hon. Mr Charles Yorke 4to
Simon Yorke of Erthig, Efq; 4to

Verses to the Memory of the
AUTHOR.

From the Magazine, *Vol* X *page* 518.

TO nobleſt Sentiments our Sorrows riſe,
   When bright diſtinguiſh'd Merit ſeeks the
     Skies.
To Virtue's ſelf the generous Tears refine
That flow, *Meliſſa!* o'er a Fate like Thine.
  O loſt too early! as too late acquir'd!
Yet, e'en thus lately, honour'd and admir'd
Tho' by no Forms of dull Acquaintance
    prov'd,
Superior Worth at once is known and lov'd,
At once with full convictive Light appears,
Nor waits the ſlow Diſcovery of Years.

  Such Worth was hers, nor dreads the vulgar
     Lot
To be at once lamented and forgot;
While in her Lines, with bright unfading Bloom,
She triumphs o'er th' Oblivion of the Tomb.
Here ever new the fair Ideas riſe,
Enchant with Beauty, and with Strength ſurpriſe;
United here the rival Graces meet
The Force of Judgment, and the Fire of Wit.
While ſofter Strokes of more affecting Art
Flow from the gentler Dictates of the Heart,
(The Whole with each engaging Charm deſign'd,)
Compleats the laſting Picture of her Mind.

To the MEMORY of a MOTHER.

From the Magazine, Vol X *p* 311

WHY finks my Heart beneath a Weight of
    Woe?
Why throbs my Breaft? my Tears inceffant flow?
Why flies the Slumber from my aching Eyes?
What prompts the Sigh when Morning gilds the
    Skies?
Day's chearful Orb, why hateful to my Sight?
Why feeks my Soul the mournful Gloom of
    Night?
Afk Death the Caufe---too well the Tyrant
    knows,
From his relentlefs Hand proceed my Woes.

To thee, bleft Shade! I chearlefs tune the Lay,
All, for thy Love, my bleeding Heart can pay,
As now that Love a fad Remembrance brings,
The Mufe muft weep---yet while fhe weeps, fhe
    fings!

How did her Care, her Tendernefs engage
The artlefs Fondnefs of my infant Age?
And when advancing in the Years of Youth
Teach me the ways of Wifdom and of Truth?
The happy Hours flew unperceiv'd along,
While native Wit flow'd, tuneful, from her
    Tongue:
Her gentle Numbers charm'd the lift'ning Ear,
MELISSA's Name was to the Mufes dear.

Na-

Nature, in her, with Care unwonted join'd
The beauteous Frame and still more beauteous
    Mind;
Neither diminish'd by affected Art,
Nor Guile deform'd, nor Pride debas'd her Heart,
Above her Sex's Foibles was her Aim,
Too just, too good, to flatter or defame;
To Friendship ever true, in Converse free,
And dear to All -- but oh! most dear to Me.
With every Virtue was her Bosom warm,
And pure Religion brighten'd ev'ry Charm.
But say, lamented Shade, should I repine
That thou hast chang'd the Mortal for Divine?
More than I've lost in thee, to thee is giv'n:
I've lost a Parent---thou hast gain'd a Heav'n.---
With spotless *Rowe* you tread th' etherial Plains,
And wake the golden *Lyre* to heav'nly Strains,
Harmonious join the blest angelick Choirs,
God all the Theme---while God the Song inspires.

    Long as I wander thro' the Maze of Life,
Amidst delusive Joys, and Cares, and Strife,
Fix'd in my Breast thy Mem'ry shall reside,
Thy Virtue fire me, and thy Precepts guide:
Thus shall I fearless feel the Hand of Death,
Like thee, in Peace, resign my trembling Breath,
My Soul exulting meet her pitying God,
And join thy Raptures in the blest Abode.

                CAROLINA.

To

To Miss CHARLOTTE BRERETON,

From the Magazine, Vol X p 618

WHILE near *Sabrina*'s limpid Stream
 I tun'd the trembling Lyre,
On that exalted awful Theme
 That kindled *Moses*' Fire;

Sudden was heard a doleful Sigh,
 The Shepherds feem'd to know;
" MELISSA grieves, the Shepherds cry,
 " May Heav'n avert her Woe "

MELISSA grieves! hark! louder Groans
 Your fond Miftake relate!
'Tis CAROLINA thus bemoans
 Her loft MELISSA's Fate.

MELISSA *taught in Years of Youth,*
 True Wisdom's Ways to prize;
Her Numbers charm'd,---her Form,---her Truth,
 But oh!-----MELISSA dies!-----

Thou dear Inchantress of the Plains,
 Thy mournful Tale give o'er,
We faint beneath thy pow'rful Strains,
 Our Souls can bear no more.

Yet fainting thus beneath thy Strains,
 One pleafing Truth we view,-----
MELISSA's better Part remains,
 MELISSA lives in You.   R. YATE.
                                    Writ-

?★★★★★★★★★★★★★★★★★★★★★★?

Written August 7, being the Anniversary of a Mother's Death.

From the Magazine, Vol XI, p 438

WHY shoots this sudden Horror thro' my
     Breast?
Whence feels my Soul this sadd'ning Weight im-
     prest!
Why brings each rolling Year this fatal Day,
To point the Worth that Fate has snatch'd away?

How, *Mem'ry!* are thy wonted Pleasures fled!
Oh say, can'st thou re-animate the Dead?
Then might'st thou hope to sooth my tortur'd
     Mind,
And wake the Joys that Time has left behind;
But feeble Comfort can'st thou *now* bestow
To stop the Force of deep-embosom'd Woe!
While Grief presents a Parent to my Sight,
My Guardian once, my Pattern and Delight!
Presents her on this sad remember'd Day,
A Form of cold inanimated Clay!
Mute is that tuneful *Tongue* that once could move
With all the Sweetness of maternal Love.
Still is the *Hand* that touch'd the tender Lyre
With all the Sense that *Wisdom* could inspire.
Low lies the *Head* replete with Learning's Store,
And that unblemish'd *Heart* shall *beat* no more!
No more that gentle *Voice* my Ear delight!
No more that well known *Face* rejoice my Sight!
                Lost

Loft all my Profpect form'd of *Blifs* to come,
And every *Hope* lies wither'd in her *Tomb*.

To me in vain her Treafures *Autumn* fpreads,
In vain the *Sun* his cheàrlefs Influence fheds !
In vain the *Trees* their taftelefs Fruitage yield,
Or golden *Harvefts* wave along the Field ,
All all to me appears one defart Coaft,
Since fhe---in whom I plac'd my Pride---is loft !

Yet fhall the conftant Mufe her Tribute bring,
The Tear fhall pay---the annual *Dirge* fhall fing !
With filial Duty bathe thy honour'd Urn,
And on this Day with *Grief diftinguifh'd* mourn.

Life's Journey now all comfortlefs I run,
Thou, my *true* Guide, and *beft* Protection gone !
Yet fhall thy *Writings*---thy *Example*, be
The *Rule* to keep my Steps from *Error* free ,
To lead me fafe to that celeftial Shore,
Where happy we fhall join---to part no more !

So when fome ev'ning Trav'ller, wearied, fpies
The *Orb* of *Light* defcend the *weftern* Skies,
With cautious Eye each Object round he views,
As faint his dubious Journey he purfues:
Anxious improves the leaft reflected Ray,
And treads with fearful Steps the dangerous Way.

CAROLINA.

To CAROLINA, *occasioned by her ingenious Poem on the Anniversary of her Mother's Death.*

From the Magazine, Vol XI. *p* 438

COu'd Tears, and Sighs, and Pray'rs recall the
  Dead,
In vain thou had'ft not wept, and figh'd, and
  pray'd:
Then ceafe at length thy unavailing Grief,
Since Tears, and Sighs, and Prayers yield no Re-
  lief.
Rather to Heav'n thy warmeft Thanks return,
That did not fooner give thee Caufe to mourn,
But lent thy Parent long to blefs thy Sight,
To warn thee from the Wrong, and teach thee
  Right,
Point out the Way to that celeftial Shore,
Where ye fhall one Day meet---to part no more.
Of Heav'n the Blefling, fay, cou'dft thou obtain,
To animate her facred Duft again?
Wou'dft thou, impell'd by thy exceffive Love,
Wifh her to quit the radiant Realms above,
Thofe blifsful Seats where Joys eternal flow,
Again to journey thro' this Vale of Woe?
Ah no, thou wou'dft not give a Mark of Love,
Thy filial Piety could ne'er approve.
What tho' no common Lofs thou didft fuftain,
Yet longer why wilt thou lament in vain?
        Enough

Enough to Nature's giv'n ; let Reafon now
Forbid the Sigh to rife, the Tear to flow.

Forgive th' officious Mufe, dejected Fair,
Who fondly feeks thy piercing Grief to fhare,
And fympathizing tries her foothing Art,
To eafe the Anguifh of thy bleeding Heart ;
By Nature taught to pity the Diftreft,
By Virtue to confole th' afflicted Breaft.

AMASIUS.

Mrs *BRERETON*'s Poems.

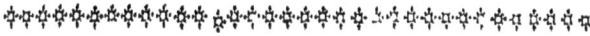

✤✤✤✤✤✤✤✤✤✤✤✤✤ ✤✤✤✤✤✤✤✤✤ ✤✤✤✤✤✤✤ ✤✤✤✤✤

Thoughts on Life, Death, Judgment, Heaven, *and* Hell.

AUTHOR of Life! Creator wife and
    Juft,
Whofe Goodnefs rais'd this Fabrick
    from the Duft,
Bade crimfon Streams thro' filver Channels glide,
And active Spirits fwell the nervous Tide ;
Thy Image ftampt on the new-moulded Clay,
And animating breath'd the vital Ray !

  To Thee, Eternal! I my Being owe,
Give me the Value of thy Gift to know.

Let me not spend the LIFE thou gav'st in vain,

But run my *Race* that I the Race obtain,

Tho' I thro' thorny Paths my Way persue,

Grant me to keep the Goal, and Prize in View;

Thro' all Life's *Warfare*, let the Christian Arms,

In every Combat shield my Soul from Harms.

The humid *Vapour* which exhales from Earth,

Owes to the Sun's attractive Warmth its Birth;

O may my Life, tho' from the Dust it springs,

Soar to " the Sun with healing in his Wings."

Tho' its Duration is like the short-liv'd *Flow'r*,

Impress upon my Mind its fading Hour;

Tho' like a *Shadow*, or a *Span*, it be,

Grant me substantial, boundless Bliss in Thee!

Tho' like Night's *Dream* it vanishes away,

O let me wake to everlasting Day!

Thy Doom I must fulfil,—resign this Breath,

And sleep, 'till summon'd in the Arms of DEATH

To

To Nature pay, the laſt great Debt I owe,

And paſs the Realms of her deteſted Foe ,

Impowr'd by Thee, her Offspring to ſubdue,

All, but thy favour'd, thy diſtinguiſh'd *Two*.

Ev'n *thy Beloved Son*, has felt his Dart,

And groan'd beneath the agonizing Smart.

What Proofs of Love, *Redeemer* ! did'ſt Thou give,

Muſt *God* ſubmit to die, that we might live !

Death's dreadful Shocks, he, for his Foll'weis, bore

And ſmooth'd that Paſſage, which was rough before

With diff'rent *Aſpects*, *Death* ('tis own'd) appears,

Horror, Deſpair, and formidable Fears,

Serpents around his Iron Sceptre roul,

Affright the guilty, unbelieving, Soul.

—But to the Faithful, and the Juſt, as mild

As the fond Nurſe, who ſooths to ſleep her Child ,

To them, he comes the Meſſenger of Peace,

His golden Sceptre Olive Branches grace.

He from Oppreſſion flees, from Care, from Pain ;

From earthly Loſs, conveys to heav'nly Gain ,

Then

Their wearied Limbs lays gently in the Tomb,
Secure from Evil, and the Wrath to come.

Reflect, my Soul! on that tremendous Day,
When the GREAT JUDGE his Glory shall display,
When the *last Trumpet's* Sound this Globe shall
   shake,
And those, who slept five thousand Years, awake
The *Earth*, th'unfathom'd *Deep*, their *Dead* resign,
And scatter'd Limbs, their ancient Bodies join;
Atoms, tho' imperceptible to Sight,
Affembled, with their kindred Duft unite,
Each Particle affumes its former Seat,
Where all their proper Functions muft repeat,
The Frame collected;—to inform the whole,
To its old Dwelling now returns the Soul ·
Embodied, to receive its final *Doom*,
A fad, or bleft Eternity to come.
" But lo ! the JUDGE, in yon ethenal Plain,
" Myriads of Spirits attendant, in his Train,
       " Than

" Than the Sun's Rays his Countenance more bright,

" His Robe, than new-fall'n Snow, a purer white ;

" Behold, around his Breast, the golden Zone,

" Behold, the flaming, the refulgent Throne ;

" Encircled by the Rainbow's various die,

" With which the brightest Emerald might vie ·

" And on his radiant Vesture, lo, the Words

" Infcrib'd, the KING OF KINGS, AND LORD OF

  " LORDS '

His awful Summons now must be obey'd,

" The Judgment fet, the Books are open laid.

All *Adam*'s Race, before the JUDGE appear,

In faithful Hope, or struck with guilty Fear.

" He, who *Believers* ranfom'd with his Blood,

" Will feparate the Wicked from the Good ;

" Those on his right falute thefe Words divine,

(While from his Eyes the Beams of Mercy fhine)

" Come my Belov'd, inherit now the Joy,

" For you prepar'd, which none can e'er deftroy,

      " For

" For I was *hungry*, and you gave me Meat,

" *Thirfty*, and you affwag'd the parching Heat ;

" A *Stranger*, and you kindly me receiv'd,

" *Naked*, you cloath'd me, *Sick*, and you reliev'd.

" In *Prifon*, and even *there*, you Vifits pay.

" O Lord! when did we this ? the Righteous fay.

" Th' *omnifcient Judge*, will gracioufly reply,

" When e'er you did the Wants of *thefe* fupply,

" To me 'twas done. And great is your Reward ;

" Receive the Kingdom, long for you prepar'd.

" To thofe on his Left Hand he thus fhall fpeak—

(While pointed Light'nings from his Eye-balls

break.)

" Ye Workers of Iniquity retire,

" Depart ye hence to everlafting Fire,

" Prepar'd for curfed Spirits, and for you,

' Who no Compaffion for your Brethren knew.

" Avenging fiends to *Tophet*, thefe convey,

" The Righteous, Angels guide to Realms of Day.

" Where

" Where as a *Bride,* magnificently dreſt

" In all the Splendour, of the radiant *Eaſt;*

" The glorious, holy *City* they behold,

" Whoſe Walls are Jaſper, and whoſe Pavements

 " Gold.

" The Saphir, its bright Azure here diſplays;

" And Amethiſts, emit their purple Rays .

" Their lucid Verdure Em'ralds here diſcloſe,

" And Topaz here its golden Luſtre ſhews ;

" The Ruby ſhines with crimſon Radiance bright;

" And the rich Diamond pours a Flood of Light.

" Angels, and Saints, round the tranſparent Throne,

" Proſtrate, adore th' Eternal, holy one,

" Praiſe, Bleſſing, Wiſdom, Pow'r, and Glory, give,

" To him who dy'd, but ſhall for ever live

" There Martyrs, `who for *Truth* had Champions

 " Gold,

" And ſeal'd their Teſtimonial with their Blood;

      " Juſt

" Juſt Men made perfect, from their Labours reſt,

" With beatifick Viſion ever bleſt.

" There they triumphant Allelujahs ſing ·

" O Grave where is thy Pow'r! O Death thy Sting!

" No Care, no Anguiſh here, no Tears, no Sighs,

" For *God* ſhall wipe all Sorrow from their Eyes,

" His Choſen to the Streams of Life ſhall lead,

" And with the Fruits of Paradiſe will feed.

" No Curſe, no Tempter, here, no Fraud, no Strife,

" They're now ſecure, beneath the *Trees of Life*.

" Nor need of *Sun*, where all 's efulgent bright,

" All *Harmony*, and *Love* and *Life*, and *Light*,

" Fulneſs of *Joy*, ineffable, divine !

" Where GOD's own Countenance ſhall ever ſhine.

Father of Mercy ! may thy *Word* and *Grace*,

Direct, and guide me to this holy Place;

Where I with heav'nly Choirs employ'd may be,

And, with theſe Eyes, my dear *Redeemer* ſee.

" All

" All who in Idols, or in Riches truſt,

" The Sorcerer, the Lewd, and the Unjuſt ;

" The Wretch who his Creator dares deny ;

" And whoſoe'er invents, or loves a Lie ;

" Far, from the *holy Preſence* muſt retire,

" To ever-living Lakes of liquid Fire.

" Where, nor the Dawns of Light, or Hope ariſe,

" Nor Flames are quench'd, nor gnawing Worm e'er

　　" dies,

" To aggravate their Woe, in Torments toſt,

" They from afar ſhall ſee the Heaven they loſt.

" For Ever loſt ! while they're condemn'd to dwell,

" With curſed Fiends, who feed the *Rage of Hell.*

" With Fury, Horror, Envy, Shame, Deſpair,

" *Eternal too !*—Oh ! who the *Thought* can bear !

C　　　　　　　　VER-

VERSES *on the Loſs of a* FRIEND.

Written in the Year 1709.

AH! happy Solitude, thrice bleſt the Day!
When in thy Shades I paſs'd my Hours away;
Exempt from Cares, retir'd from public Noiſe,
Nought to prevent, or interrupt my Joys:
No anxious Fears my Quiet to moleſt,
No Storms to diſcompoſe my *Halcyon* Breaſt;
Not Love, Ambition, Pride, or female Strife,
Serene each Thought and blameleſs as my Life.

Oft have I lonely rang'd the verdant Fields,
To view the Glories which the Summer yields,
How beauteous *Flora* decks the fruitful Earth,
Producing daily ſome delightful Birth.
Here all that's fair, that's beautiful, or ſweet,
The Lilly, Roſe, and purple Vi'let meet,
And ſeem enamell'd round my happy Feet.

Thro'

Thro' smiling Meads, there, *Alyn* gently glides,

And paints with fragant Pride its fertile Sides;

In wild *Meanders* runs its wanton Maze,

Winding its Streams a thousand various Ways.

Oft have I sate, and in the cooling Shade,

Sung to the Murmurs which its Waters made.

Tagus, *Pactolus* too, I thought to be,

Meer Puddles, *Alyn* ! when compar'd with Thee !

That celebrated *Heliconian* Spring,

The sacred Fountain where the Muses sing,

Could not appear more pleasing to my Sight,

Than chrystal *Alyn* !—Oh ! the vast Delight !

When to thy flow'ry Bank some Book I brought,

Stor'd with rich Wit, with useful Knowledge

      fraught.

There I the feather'd Choristers might hear,

Warbling their Notes to entertain my Ear.

Poor *Philomela* ! tunes her solemn Strains,

Of *Tereus*, still she mournfully complains;

While all the feather'd Tribes around her throng,
And liften to her foft harmonious Song,
Then warble out their Plaudit.—Thus each Senfe
Is treated without Danger, or Expence.
The Meads delightful to the Eye appear,
The Birds with Mufick foothe the ravifh'd Ear;
Rich Fruit, cool Streams, and odorif'rous Scent,
At once the Tafte, the Touch, and Smell content.
To crown all this, and make my Joys compleat,
A Friend I had near this belov'd Retreat;
So well we lov'd, fo faithful and fo true,
That mutual were the Joys or Pains we knew.
Thus liv'd we, like our early Parents, free
From Fears or Cares, in fweet Simplicity
Till by a moft unhappy turn of Fate,
We loft our *Eden*, our contented State,
For Love the falfe feducing Serpent play'd,
And foon beguil'd the fond believing Maid,
Too foon, Alas! her eafy Heart betray'd.

Pray'rs, Tears, Entreaties, all in vain did prove;

Neglected Friendſhip muſt ſubmit to Love.

Yet ſoon ſhe mourn'd the fatal Step ſhe made,

I left to ſhare a Grief I could not aid!

Grown thus forlorn by her unguarded Choice,

Her hapleſs Fortune damp'd my former Joys;

Of all their former Pleaſures now bereft,

At laſt reſolv'd—the once dear Plains I left,

With Friendſhip all my ſweet Contentment flew!

I croſt o'er *Dee*, and bade the Shades, Adieu!

To M---TH---W W----M----LD, *Eſq;*
near Wantage.

T? expreſs her Thanks, and at your Friend's
Command,

Again *Meliſſa* takes the Pen in Hand,

Hopes this will find, that all are well with You;

While we jog on,—juſt as we us'd to do.

When

When the Squire rifes from his Bed forlorn,

He fteers his Courfe to Fields of rip'ning Corn :

Or to the verdant Meads he takes his Way,

Where jocund Lads, and Laffes tofs the Hay.

But how, or wherefoe'er the Morn is fpent,

At Noon we meet, by general Confent,

Then on a good *Sheep's Arm** or *knighted* Loyn,

Plain fimple Commons—cheerfully we dine.

Whene'er the Breaft of Mutton does appear,

We wifh, good Miftrefs *Wymondfold* was here.

In Red, or White (to *Beech's* fure Advantage)

We toaft the Church, and King—and Friends near

　　Wantage.

Sometimes when all engage in high Debate,

I ftand as Champion for the Marriage State ;

And for my Boldnefs, plead your late Commiffion,

To footh, or fright him, to your bleft Condition.

　　　　　　　　　　　　　　　Vain

* The *Welfh* call a Shou'der of Mutton a *Sheep's Arm*, and a Ca-
pon a *Cock Gelding*

Vain are my Reasons! he's not mov'd a Jot;

Sometimes indeed he'll answer, sometimes not.

I may harangue, till I've quite crack'd my Voice;

I much suspect he'll ne'er approve my Choice.

Therefore no more this Matter I'll persue;

I'm certain none can hit his Taste like you.

Chuse for your Friend as for yourself you chose,

And be assur'd, you won't your Labour lose;

Find you a Fair exactly like your Lady,

With Hand, and Heart, I'll answer he'll be ready.

This I sincerely wish with Heart most fervent:

Who am to you and yours,

An humble Servant.

P. S. The Squire was *quick* enough to catch

the *Joke,*

The Pipes at *Chester* were before bespoke,

Neat are the Tubes and Bole of purest white;

And my *Epistles,* Sir, will serve to *light.*

· **To**

To D A M O N.

I.

CEafe, *Damon*, ceafe I'll hear no more:
　Your fulfom Flattery give o'er;
I fcorn this mean fallacious Art,
By which you'd fteal, not win my Heart:
In me it never can Compaffion move,
And fooner will Averfion raife than Love.

II.

If you to Love would me incline,
Affert the Man, forbear to whine;
Let Time, and plain Sincerity,
And faithful Love your Pleaders be:
For, truft me, *Damon*, if thofe fail,
Thefe fervile wheedling Tricks will ne'er prevail.

To PHILOTIMUS.

I

PHilotimus, if you'd approve
   Yourself a faithful Lover,
You muſt no more my Anger move,
But in the mildeſt Terms of Love,
   Your Paſſion ſtill diſcover.

II.

Tho' born to rule, you muſt ſubmit
   To my Commands with Awe ,
Nor think your Sex can you acquit,
For *Cupid*'s Empire won't admit,
   Nor own a *Salique* Law.

EPIGRAM.

TIS eaſier much to kindle Satire's Fire,
   Than a juſt Light to ſhew what we admire,
Satires, like Wild-fires, from rank Soils ariſe ,
Praiſes, like Sun-beams, ſhine from kindred Skies

D   *The*

The 9th ODE of the 3d Book of HORACE. *Imitated.*

HE.

WHILE I alone poffefs'd your Love,
 And reign'd unrival'd in your Breaft,
No Mortal greater Joy could prove,
 Nor *Jove* himfelf could be more Bleft.

SHE.

While to my Eyes alone you bow'd,
 And own'd me Queen of your Defires;
The Queen of Heav'n was ne'er fo proud,
 Tho' fhe with Love great *Jove* infpires.

HE.

To *Cloe*'s pow'rful Voice and Wit,
 My Heart is now a willing Slave;
For whom to die I would fubmit,
 If that her dearer Life could fave.

SHE

SHE.

Young *Damon* now 's my only Care,

   Who meets my Flame with tend'reft Truth ;

For whom a double Death I'd bear,

   If Fate would fpare the lovely Youth.

HE.

What if my former Flame renews,

   And I renounce fair *Cloe*'s Charms,

Would you young *Damon* then refufe,

   And me receive in thofe dear Arms?

SHE.

Tho' thou fo rough, fo pettifh art,

   Tho' he fo gentle, gay and trim;

So firm thou'rt fix'd in this fond Heart,

   I'd die with thee, ere live with him.

The

✤✤✤✤✤✤✤✤✤✤✤✤✤✤✤✤✤✤✤✤✤✤✤✤✤✤✤✤✤✤✤✤✤✤✤

The 5th ODE of the 4th Book of Horace
imitated, and apply'd to the King. 1716.

I.

O Thou! whom Heav'n's propitious Pow'r
    Ordain'd to do fair *Britain* Right,
Her ancient Luftre to reftore,
    Return! and glad her longing Sight:
Return, great Prince! and grace our Ifle
    With thy aufpicious Rays;
Her Sun to welcome Thee will fmile,
    And fhine in brighter Days.

II.

As our fond Sex, all drown'd in Tears,
    For their long-abfent Sons complain;
They Heav'n alarm with Vows and Pray'rs,
    With wifhful Eyes look o'er the Main:
Nor will they from the Shore remove,
    But ftill impatient mourn,
Thus *Britain* pines with loyal Love,
    'Till her great Lord return.

The

III.

The Lafs now jocund milks our Kine,
 Which we fecurely grazing view;
Our publick Fears we now refign,
 And our domeftick Care renew:
The Merchant plows the briny Flood
 To fetch us rich Brocades;
And *Carolina*, great and good,
 To virtuous Life perfuades.

IV.

That Juftice now refumes her Sword,
 And with an equal Balance weighs,
That Vice begins to be abhor'd,
 'Tis *George* alone deferves the Praife!
Happy in Honours thou haft won,
 Bleft in thy Royal Race!
While we contemplate in thy Son
 Thy Virtue, and thy Face.

Who

V.

Who fears the falſe rapacious *Scot* ?

   The *French*: the *Swede*'s romantick Pride ?

Who dreads what tripple Mitres plot?

   While *George* and Heav'n eſpouſe our Side :

While he is ſafe, we're free from Harms,

   And void of female Fears,

No anxious Thoughts impair our Charms,

   Or dim our Eyes with Tears.

VI.

To Thee our pureſt Wiſhes flow,

   To Thee our grateful Songs are due;

Religion, Liberty, we owe

   To great *Naſſau*, and greater You !

Long, long may you our Iſle adorn,

   While all confeſs your gentle Sway ;

Theſe are our Toilet Vows each Morn,

   And theſe each Ev'ning crown our Tea.

VERSES *occafioned by reading the fore-going* ODE. *By Mr* HINCHLIFFE.

I.

WHEN fam'd *Auguftus* rul'd the *Roman* State,

And blefs'd the World with his indulgent

Sway.;

Around his Throne did all the Mufes wait,

The Monarch's Worth and Glory to difplay.

II.

Then, lift'ning *Tyber* heard th' *Horatian* Lyre,

His mighty Mafter's godlike Acts rehearfe

The *Mantuan's* Bofom glow'd with hallow'd Fire,

Raifing his Patron in immortal Verfe.

III.

But lo! a greater than *Auguftus* reigns

O'er our more happy, yet ungrateful Land'

Oh' let the Mufe divine, with facred Strains,

The Madnefs of an impious Age withftand.

'Tis

IV.

'Tis done,—*Meliſſa* wakes the warbling Strings,

Hark! how the loyal Fair, in ſofteſt Lays,

The firſt of Men! and beſt of Princes! ſings,

Teaching her ſweet-tun'd Harp our Sov'reign's lofty

Praiſe.

To the Author of the foregoing VERSES.

I.

INgenious Bard! when you inſpire,

And urge to ſing our Sov'reign's Fame;

I quit my Needle, ſtring my Lyre,

And boldly dare the mighty Theme.

II.

While female Rebels plague our Iſle,

Quite loſt to Virtue, Senſe, or Shame;

While theſe the beſt of Kings revile,

My Loyalty I'll thus proclaim.

Their

III.

Their noify Malice I defpife !
  Too oft, alas! the Triflers prove,
They're guided only by *Caprice*,
  Alike in Loyalty, and Love.

IV.

Oh! cou'd *Meliffa* fing like you !
  Aloft, her tow'ring Mufe fhould rife ;
Our mighty Monarch's Praife perfue,
  And lift his Name above the Skies.

V.

In *George*, the Fire of *Britifh* Kings
  Does with *Sophia*'s Sweetnefs joyn ;
From her this heav'nly Goodnefs fprings
  That makes the Hero half divine.

VI.

Sophia ! virtuous, learn'd and fair !
  Whofe Death each Grace, each Mufe would grieve,
Had we not *Carolina* here,
  In whom her fhining Virtues live.

E   But

VII.

But oh! where roves the giddy Mufe,

   Unequal to the wond'rous Theme,

Do thou the glorious Subject chufe,

   And give Eternity to Fame.

VIII.

I feel the Woman now prevail,

   I feel, I want thy manly Fire *!*

I feel my Strings, and Numbers fail,

   I'll ceafe .—and filently admire.

✤✤✤✤✤✤✤✤✤✤✤✤✤✤✤✤✤✤✤✤✤✤✤✤✤✤✤✤✤✤✤✤✤✤✤✤

On the K I N G's Return.

In Imitation of the Fourteenth Ode of Horace.

GREAT *George* return'd ' awake my Lyre '
   Let that lov'd Name the Strings infpire,

Let Vales the joyful Notes refound,

And gladden all the Hills around !

Brigh

Bright *Carolina*, Royal Fair !
Hafte to the aweful Dome of Pray'r ;
With all your beauteous Train, adore
The Powers who fafe our King reftore.

And you, chafte Wives' due Thanks prefent'
Whofe Mates t' attend the Hero went ,
Forbear your Sighs, difplay your Charms,
They now return to blefs your Arms !

O welcome, welcome facred Prince !
Thou guardian Care of Providence,
Now you return to blefs our Ifle,
We fweetly fing, and gaily fmile.

Oh ! happy, happy, happy we'
Bleft with great *George* and Liberty '
In Mercy *George* to *Britain* given '
George the fov'reign Gift of Heaven '

Let

Let all with grateful Joy abound,
With Plenty let the Board be crown'd ;
Go, skim the Cream-bowl, bring the Tea,
To Mirth we'll dedicate this Day.

To Nehemiah Griffith, *Esq;*
Author of the Leek.

WHEN you, O *Briton!* our pass'd Woes relate,
My Soul grows anxious for my Country's
Fate ;
Sighs rend my Breast, my Eyes dissolve in Tears,
And all the Woman's Tenderness appears.

But when you change the melancholy Scene,
And shew us happy under *George's* Reign ;
Display the Glories of the Royal Line,
And celebrate our matchless *Wihelmine :*

Elate

Elate with Joy, my Heart in Tranſport ſprings !
I bleſs the Bard, that ſo divinely ſings !

The Saint * looks down propitious from above,
And does with Smiles our Happineſs approve ;
Pleas'd with the Verſe, you to his Memory pay,
And the bright Dame that dignifies his Day †
So ſtrong your Senſe, ſo ſweet your Numbers flow,
He ſtops his Lyre,—to hear you ſing below !

Let *Carolina* ſtill inſpire thy Lays,
Till our glad Hills learn to reſound her Praiſe ;
What more could *Wales* deſire, or Heav'n allow,
Than She our *Princeſs* ' and our Poet *Thou* ʾ

E PIS-

---

* St *David*, Patron of *Wales*   † 1ſt of *March*

EPISTLE *to Mrs* ANNE GRIFFITHS,

Written from London, *in* 1718.

MY beft lov'd Friend ! fince ravifh'd from thy
        Sight,

I've known no Joy, no Comfort, nor Delight ;

But ftill to meagre Care, and Grief, a Prey,

Am tofs'd about in Life's tempeftuous Sea !

If ought has Pow'r my anxious Mind to eafe,

'Tis the Rememb'rance of thofe happy Days,

Thofe dear, thofe blifsful Days, I pafs'd with You,

Blifsful indeed !—but too too foon they flew !

And now the fad Alternative I feel,

I've had the Good, and muft endure the Ill !

Abandon'd thus to Woe, what can I fend

But tedious dull Complaints to Thee my Friend ?

Unbofom all my Grief, impart my Care,

To that dear Breaft that bears a friendly Share ?

Ah,

Ah, Friend ! what Storms, what Tryals have I pafs'd,

Since you and I embrac'd each other laft !

But ftay—why fhould I now repeat my Moan,

To Thee my Suff'rings are already known.

Juft Heaven that fees, may make my Sorrows ceafe;

And we may meet once more in Joy and Peace.

Truft we to that—mean while I fain would fay,

Something to drive thefe gloomy Thoughts away :

For this, I call the long neglected Mufe ;

But fhe her wonted Kindnefs does refufe ;

Capricious grown fhe follows Fortune's Train,

Nor longer with th' unhappy will remain.

Where Melancholy reigns, fhe fcorns to ftay ;

But ftill attends the Great, the Rich, the Gay.

'Tis fo ; 'twas fo of old , this *Nafo* found,

Whofe Brows with facred Bays had oft been crown'd:

While yet at *Rome*, approv'd, carefs'd by All,

Th' obfequious Mufes ftill obey'd his Call;

"Of

" Of Bodies chang'd to other Forms he sung,

This smooth'd the Verse, and that the Lyre new

    strung :

Around the Bard officiously they throng,

And bear him thro' the vast advent'rous Song !

But, when in Exile he to, sing essay'd,

Not one of all the Nine would grant her Aid !

The witty *Terence*, in dramatic Strains,

From list'ning *Rome* a just Applause obtains,

How lively are the Comic Scenes he penn'd,

While Fortune smil'd, and *Lelius* was his Friend !

But soon as these their Favours once withdrew,

The Muse deny'd her kind Assiftance too !

If *Horace* such Misfortunes had sustain'd,

His sprightly Vein he ne'er could have maintain'd :

But blest with all an Epicure could charm !

His Flocks, his Herds, and his delicious Farm ;

His bounteous Patron, and his noble Friends,

And every Joy that Luxury attends :

Unvex'd

Unvex'd with Troubles, and exempt from Fear,

He owns himfelf the Gods peculiar Care ·

And thus fecur'd from Want (moft gravely wife ')

Inftructs, declaims, and Fortune's Pow'r defies.

But had he once to Poverty been brought,

The Bard had wanted many a brighter Thought !

A plenteous eafy Life, and profp'rous State,

Gay fmiling Mirth and chearful Thoughts create :

Thofe Gifts, tho' to a mod'rate Genius join'd,

Brighten the Fancy and elate the Mind.

But fhou'd fome fnarling Critic chance to view

Thefe undigefted Lays defign'd for you;

The furly Blade, methinks, would ftorm and fume ;

" How dares this filly Woman thus prefume,

" In her crude injudicious Lines to name

" Thofe ancient Poets of immortal Fame ?

" The Women, now forfooth' are Authors grown,

" And write fuch Stuff our Sex would blufh to own !

That

That I am dull, is what I own and know;
But why I may'nt be privileg'd to fhew
That Dullnefs to a private Friend or two,
(As to the World Male Writers often do)
I can't conceive:—Dullnefs alone's my Fault;
Guiltlefs of impious Jeft, or obfcene Thought!
None e're can fay that I have loofely writ,
Nor would at that dear Rate be thought a Wit.
Fair Modefty was once our Sex's Pride,
But fome have thrown that bafhful Grace afide·
The *Behns*, the *Manleys* head this motley Train,
Politely lewd and wittily prophane;
Their Wit, their fluent Style (which all muft own)
Can never for their Levity atone.
But Heaven that ftill its Goodnefs to denote,
For every Poifon gives an Antidote,
Firft our *Orinda*, fpotlefs in her Fame,
As chafte in Wit, refcu'd our Sex from Shame·

And

And now, when *Heywood's* foft feducing Style
Might heedlefs Youth and Innocence beguile,
Angelic Wit, and pureft Thoughts agree,
In tuneful *Singer*, and great *Winchelfea.*

For me, who never durft to more pretend
Than to amufe myfelf, and pleafe my Friend ,
If fhe approves of my unskilful Lays ;
I dread no Critic, and defire no Praife.
Oh, how I long with you to pafs the Day,
Sedately chearful, innocently gay !
Where *Alyn* glides, to breathe my native Air,
To view our pleafant Hills, and dear * *Moelgaer.*

But fince thefe flatt'ring Hopes now difappear,
And Tyes too potent will detain me here ;
Thy rural Pleafures for a while fufpend,
Oh! come and comfort thy dejected Friend !

F 2   Thy

* A Mountain in *Denbighfhire.*

Thy Prefence only can afford Relief,

Reftore my Peace of Mind, and heal my Grief.

Thy joyous Converfe will my Cares beguile,

And this fad Face fhall learn again to fmile!

To Mrs A. GRIFFITH.

With fome Poems.

DEAR to my Soul, and Sharer in my Heart,
    Accept the Trifles which I here impart.

Imagine not, in Vanity, I fend

Such worthlefs Toys, to fuch a worthy Friend.

'Tis to perform the Promife early made,

That all I wrote, fhou'd at your Feet be laid.

Some I ftill lofe, but what the Mufe fecures,

Is, as the Writer,

very humbly Tours.

April 7, 1733.

On

On seeing Mrs ELIZ. OWEN, *now Lady*
   Longueville, *in an embroider'd Suit,*
   all her own Work.

SURE, this glorious Lady's the fair Queen of
      May !
Tho' a Goddess, e'en F*lora* was never so gay,
With her Robe adorn'd, with the brighteſt of
     Flow'rs,
Which enamel the Meads, or encircle the Bow'rs.
Had *Eliza* been seen by the Folks of old *Rome*,
They had sworn 'twas the Goddeſs appear'd in her
     Bloom ;
At the Sight of her Garments with Flow'rets ſtrew'd
     o'er,
From gazing, and wond'ring—they'd bow and adore.

  Behold, with what Skill ſhe has damask'd the Roſe !
The charming Carnation how crimſon'd it glows !
There

There, the Lilly difclofes its fnowy white Head,
And here, their rich Purple the Violets fpread,
In fine Party-colours the Tulip is fhown,
The Jonquills, and Jeff'mines appear newly blown.
Th' Auricula, there, its Perfection difplays,
And here, bright Anemonies glorioufly blaze.

So fair a Creation, the Work of her Hands,
Firft attracts my Regard, then my Wonder commands·
So verdant the Ground is, the Flow'rs are fo gay,
In the Midft of *December*, you'd fwear it was *May!*
When thus we behold her, we needs muft confefs,
Her Fancy and Judgment are feen in her Drefs,
In her Converfe, good Senfe, and good Humour we
  find,
And own her fine Outfide excell'd by her Mind.

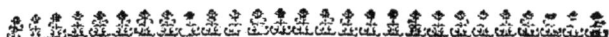

To *Lady* WILLIAMS, *and Mrs* A. DA-VIES *at* Llanoorda.

A Rambling BALLAD.

To the Tune of the Abbot *of* Canterbury.

A S I at my Window, one Day, was reflecting
 Of this thing, of that, and the other projecting,
(Tho', of what I then thought, I can give no Account)
I cast up my Eyes, and beheld the fair Mount.

     Derry down, &c.

When the Mount I beheld, it put me in Mind
Of the prudently witty, th' ingeniously kind :
" Within yonder Walls I oft cheerful have been,
" I wish the dear Ladies were now safe within.

     Derry down, &c.

How readily then the Ascent I wou'd climb !
(Much readier than raise my Style to sublime)

     When

When arriv'd at the Door, I gently wou'd rap,

For Fear of difturbing my good Lady's Nap.

Derry down,&c.

But the Sound of the Rap has quite ruin'd my

Theme,

And made me perceive I was but in a Dream,

Before I cou'd enter into the fair Dome,

I found I ftood ftill at my Window at Home.

Derry down, &c.

And is it not thus, that in Life we do fare,

When fome darling Object takes up our whole Care?

Borne high by our Hopes, which we think Fate will

crown,

Some Whim, or fome Accident, tumbles us down.

Derry down, &c.

But now moralizing afide I muft lay,

And, if it is poffible, try to be gay,

Tho'

Tho' my Lady as yet ha'n't Leave to come hither:

O *Hymen* ! O *Hymen*! how ftrong is thy *Tether*.

      Derry down, &c.

But I wifh her now here, becaufe I dare fay,

Such Sights fhe might fee, fhe can't fee every Day;

Fine Shows to our Fair, and ftrange Creatures are

  come,

And Folks call'd to fee them by Trumpet and Drum.

      Derry down, &c.

They're marvelous Sights, within Doors, no Doubt,

Tho' I'm humbly content to behold them, without;

'Tis fure no Injuftice to gaze at the Sample,

And follow the Dean of St *Patrick's* Example.

      Derry down, &c.

There has been a Cuftom for Time out of Mind,

Which will be kept up by the grateful and kind,

     G   Some

Some Token to send, from a Fair, or a Wake,

To keep, or to wear, for the kind Giver's fake.

Derry down, &c.

Theie are now at our Fair a Thoufand fine Things,

As Penknives, and Inkhorns, and charming GlafsRings,

Choice Buckles, and Bodkins, and Thimbles and

  Sciffars,

Befides a whole Shop, that's made up in the Tweezers

Derry down, &c.

But of thofe Sorts of Toys the Ladies have Plenty,

And I doubt both my Judgment, and Rhino are

  fcanty,

To chufe what is neat, or beftow many Pence,—

Quoth the Mufe, 'prithee fend them a Fairing of Senfe

Derry down, &c.

A Fairing of Senfe! how fimple the Thought!

'Tis what they don't want, and what cannot be bought

         The

They have more than enough; and furely thou'lt grant,
I little can fpare what I fo vifibly want.

Derry down, &c.

Convinc'd of this Truth;—I defign'd to withdraw,
When the Mufe flily wheedl'd me with an old Saw;
There's Love in a Nut, quoth fhe, and it may be,
Thy Love in a Ballad may pleafe my good Lady.

Derry down, &c,

Soon caught—I determin'd a Ballad to write,
I took up my Pen, and began to endite,
I'll now to my Lady, and dear Madam *Anne*,
Endeavour to fcrible the Beft that I can.

Derry down, &c.

Dear Ladies, I hope this will find you in
    Health,
In Eafe, and Contentment, in Pleafure, and Wealth;

G 2

In

In Pleafure and Wealth! oh! it were moft delighting,

Cou'd I add—as I am, at this prefent Writing.

Derry down, &c

And when will your Ladyfhip come to the Mount?

Till I fee you both there, each Minute I'll count;

Each Minute as tedious and long will appear,

As if 'twere a Month; or indeed a whole Year.

Derry down, &c.

Does not Mrs *Davies* long for the old Spot ?

And pray what new Books has your Ladyfhip got?

—I thought fomething brighter than this, I cou'd

    fay;

But the Mufe is a Jilt—for fhe's flown quite away!

Derry down, &c.

'Tis thus that fhe oft has feduc'd me to write,

And when She 'as engag'd me, fhe proves a meer Bite.

I now

I now cou'd refolve to believe her no more;
—But fuch Refolutions I've oft broke before.

Derry down, &c.

—Sure a Tumult I hear, or fome turbulent Gang !
I find 'tis a Hawker the Mob does harangue;
" For a Ha'penny here, four Songs you may buy,"
Oh! who wou'd write Ballads ! enrag'd, then I cry.

Derry down, &c.

But foon I confider'd my Ballad was new;
And, Ladies, fhou'd firft be prefented to you,
While its quite Spick and Span, frefh out of the
      Mint;
And that muft atone,—for the Nothingnefs in't.

Derry down, &c.

Shou'd any one ask what my Ballad's about,
Apollo, or my Lady, cou'd fcarce find it out;

'Tis

'Tis a kind of a Patchwork; I own amongſt Friends,
A new ſort of Sonnet of Odds and of Ends.

Derry down, &c.

If I truly do gueſs at what I intend,
Tho' my Ballad is odd, a Fairing's my End ;
I wiſh I cou'd make it, and write it in Order,
But fit to be ſeen, and tun'd at *Llanoo ᵈar.*

Derry down, &c

Cou'd I manage my Odds, and Ends, to account,
Like a Piece of Patchwork I've ſeen at the Mount,
Where Nature is copy'd ſo perfectly well,
We doubt whether Nature, or Art doth excell.

Derry down, &c.

The Ground's always verdant, and, thro' the whole
  Year,
The Lilly, the Roſe, in full Beauty apppear;

        Auriculas,

Auriculas, Vi'lets, and Jeff'mines in Bloom,

Carnations, and Tulips, enamel the Room.

Derry down, &c.

Not brighter the Colours in *Iris*'s Bow,

Not fairer the Flowers which *Flora* can ſhew;

Not *Ceres*'s Horn with more Plenty is grac'd,

Not *Minerva* herſelf cou'd 'em better have plac'd.

Derry down, &c.

Let thoſe who believe not, go thither and view,

They'll find what I ſay, for a Ballad too true;

And own, the fine Work of ſuch delicate Fingers

Shou'd be ſung by the Poets,—not by Ballad-
    Singers.

Derry down, &c.

But now to my Subject,—my Subject, God wot!

And what I intended, I've almoſt forgot.

—Will

—Will dear Lady *Williams*, and good Mrs *Davies*,

From their Humble Servant be pleas'd to receive

    This ?

                        Derry down, &c.

  'Tis not very pretty, I freely muſt own ;

But 'tis what I fancy'd, and choſe when alone :

It might have been better, had the Muſe given Aid;

But She's a ſad Jilt,—as before I have ſaid.

                        Derry down, &c.

  But to recommend it, I boldly declare,

That ſuch can't be purchas'd throughout the whole

    Fair;

I hope then my Fairing in Kindneſs you'll take,

And read it, and ſing it, for the poor Author's

    Sake.

                        Derry down, &c.

Wrexham, March 17, 1732.

To CYNTHIO.

In Imitation of the Thirty third ODE *of the first Book of* Horace.

CEASE, gen'rous *Cynthio*, ceafe to mourn !
    And let the proud *Eliza*'s Scorn
    No more thy Anger move .
No more in foft Complaints declare,
The giddy injudicious Fair
    Prefers a meaner Love.

The beauteous *Cloe Damon* loves ;
But he *Corinna* more approves,
    Though ftock'd with much Ill-nature,
While fhe regardlefs of his Sighs,
As he from *Cloe*, from him flies
    T' embrace another Creature.

H   Thus

Thus cruel Love maintains his Sway '
The Rich, the Mean, the Rude, the Gay,
    Unequal he infnares .
In vain or Senfe or Merit pleads,
In vain fincereft Truth perfuades;
    He laughs at all our Cares '

E'en I this mad Caprice have prov'd,
When gentle Youths admir'd and lov'd,
    And did my Grace implore
Ill-natur'd *Gynton* I receive,
Rough as the wild *Hibernian* Wave,
    That beats our *Cambrian* Shore!

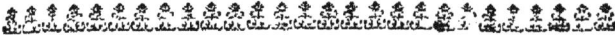

To NEHEMIAH GRIFFITH, *Esq*;

In Imitation of Horace. *Ode* III. *Book* II.

WHATE'ER, my Friend, the Heavens de-
cree!
Preferve thy Mind ferene and free !
Amidft the Calm of profp'rous State;
Amidft the Storm of adveife Fate;
Let not or Joy or Grief controul
Thy fteady firm unfhaken Soul.

If Difappointment's racking Fear,
Or Lofs of Fortune you muft bear ,
And, what yet more your Heart would move,
The Lofs of Friends or Her you love,
Or, blefs'd with Plenty, Mirth and Eafe,
You gently fpend your blifsful Days ,

Lull'd

Lull'd with foft Thoughts, fupinely laid
Beneath the Laurel's friendly Shade.

'Tis all a Cafe — Life flies away,
And here we have not long to ftay !

Then guard thy Mind from baneful Care,
T' improve thy Country Seat prepare ;
Let Oak, and Elm, and Afh arife,
A Shelter from inclement Skies:
Nor think the Task too mean to rear,
And graft, the Cherry, Peach, and Pear .
Ne'er wifh for ought beyond thy Pow r,
Enjoy with Thanks the prefent Hour !

A little while, my Friend, and you
Muft bid thefe pleafing Scenes adieu '
Thy Meadows, by whofe fertile Sides,
The chryftal *Alyn* gently glides ;

Thy Fields, thy Woods, thou muſt reſign,

And *Rhuall* be no longer thine.

Noꞇ will it much avail, if here

In ſplendid Greatneſs you appear ·

Or if you muſt thoſe Views forego,

And lead a Life obſcurely low

'Tis all alike, ſince nought can ſave,

Or gain a Reſpite from the Grave .

Each in his Turn muſt yield his Breath,

And own the Pow'r of conqu'ring Death !

ﾟﾟﾟﾟﾟﾟﾟﾟﾟﾟﾟﾟﾟﾟﾟﾟﾟﾟﾟﾟﾟﾟ

To Mr THOMAS GRIFFITH, *at the Uni-verſity of* Glaſgow.

Written in London, 1720.

YOU, Friend, who whilome toſs'd the Ball ;

Or made th' erected Nine-pin fall,

Who at the Shuffle-board were buſy,

Or ran a Race with little *Lucy* ,

Are now obfervant of the Rules,
And learned Precepts of the Schools,
Grown perfect Mafter in Difpute,
Propound, difcufs, prove, or confute :
In Terms of Art can make appear,
('Gainft Reafons ftrong that interfere,)
A foppifh Coxcomb's, no Baboon,
Nor yet a Hog, a Highland Loon ;
Tho' all your Logick you muft ufe,
To prove a Matter fo abftrufe.

Sometimes, your harrafs'd Mind t'unbend,
You chat an Hour with Whiggifh Friend,
In penfive Mood fteal out unfpy'd,
To fetch a Walk by pleafant *Clyde*
Or throw off your fcholaftick Air,
T' amufe yourfelf among the Fair,
Where for one *Meggy* you diftinguifh,
You vow you'd all the Sex relinquifh.

Sometimes you fee a Highland Beau
Come trading down to Land call'd Low
His Durk laid by, the bonny Younker,
By Dint of Argument would conquer.
In Time he'll learn to make fine Speeches,
To read, and write,—and put on Breeches.

But now, methinks, I hear you fay,
" *Meliffa* ftill is wond'rous gay !"—
I ftrive with Patience to endure
The Evils which I cannot cure.
I live fecluded from the Town,
I know but few, by few am known ;
I feldom go to Park, or Play,
And once a Fortnight drink my Tea.
Needle, or Book 'twixt Thumb and Finger,
Till tuneful Voice of Ballad-finger
Will, fometimes, make me throw it by,
And to the Window fwiftly fly.

From

From thence I hear the tatter'd Dame,
To dirty Mob, extoll the Fame
" Of Glorious *Charles* of *Swedeland*'"

Soon fhe begins another Note,
(But firft fhe hems, to clear her Throat,)
In Praife of *Jemmy*, that Knight-Errant,
Whom fome ftill *Ormond* call, I warrant!
That Rival of Great *Sweden*'s Fame,
And were his Fate to be the fame,
I will prefume 'twould granted be
He'd leave enow as wife as He.
But while fhe quaver'd out her Song,
Surrounded by the gaping Throng;
Dire Fate ' a Wagg among the Croud,
Pretending Fear, thus cry'd aloud,
" Yonder is Juftice *Brereton* coming,"
At this poor *Moll* fcarce keeps from running ;
She fneeks away, the Mob difperfe,
And fo concludes this paltry Farce.

With

With Girls, and Maids on Evening fair,

In *Tuttle-fields*, I take the Air ;

Or fometimes to the *Mill-bank* go,

From thence I hear embroider'd Beau,

And Belle in Garden-fatin dreft,

With Gallantry exchange a Jeft,

In Language as polite, and neat,

As e'er was us'd in *Billinfgate.*

Methinks, my Cafe you now deplore,

" No Lady-vis'tants as of Yore ;

" No cheerful inoffenfive Chat,

" Of Books, and Wit, of th's and that!

" What an infipid Life you lead,

" 'Twere better you in *Wales* had ftay'd."

I hate, dear Coz, to wafte the Day,

In prating Scandal, fipping Tea;

The ancient Cuftom I would chufe,

When two good Meals was all in Ufe:

I

Not

Not Toper-like, from Morn 'till Night,

Indulge my Sloth and Appetite.

Once, (and but once,) your fcribbling Friend

On high-flown Lady did attend ;

Some of the modifh Clafs foon came,

To pay their Vifits to the Dame

With Scandal, Treafon, Coffee, Tea,

The Time pafs'd merrily away.

Such was their Malice, fuch their Pride,

They *Carolina*'s felf decry'd

Then Mafquerade, Intrigue, and Drefs,

And all the trifling gay Excefs

Of Equipage, rich Jewels, Rings,

Expenfive Toys, and Gew-gaw Things,

Were next th' elab'rate Themes on which,

With much Redundancy of Speech,

The Dames harangu'd, till tir'd at laft,

I, to my dearer Jewels, hafte ;

Dearer to me than coftly Gem,

Or lac'd Gallant can be to them.

When

When gloomy Thoughts poffefs my Head,
I pay my Vifits to the Dead ;
Nought like the Abbey pleafes then,
And Monuments of famous Men.
This Head with Victor Lawrel crown'd,
Thofe Brows poetick Bays have bound ;
The glorious Warrior, and the Wit,
Muft both to Death's dire Stroke fubmit.
But here, I frankly muft confefs,
The Hero does affect me lefs
Than facred Bard .   One gains a Name,
But 'tis the other ftamps his Fame.
E'en *Marlb'rough* whofe Renown excells
The Tales which ancient Story tells
Of Demy-gods, his Name would die,
And Deeds in dark Oblivion lie ;
But that an *Addifon* conveys
Immortal Verfe to future Days,

In

In which his Acts will be read o'er,
Till this vaft Globe fhall be no more.`
That Monument of wond'rous Frame,
Rais'd by an Emp'ror to his Fame,
Devouring Time can wafte away;
But facred Verfe will ne'er decay.

Perhaps, you think to hear from me,
How Whiggs, and Tories now agree;
The high-flown Sparks in a Bravado,
Threaten'd us with a ftrong Armado:
They boafted much of Men, and Money,
Would come from *Mach'vell Alberony*.
But Difappointment, and Defpair,
Have made them look like what they are.
The Dons may blefs the ftormy Weather,
That ftop'd their Fleet from coming hither;
For had they come, the *Hogan Mogan*,
And *Britons* led by brave *Cadogan*,

Wou'd foon have made them wifh in vain,

They ne'er had left their native *Spain*.

—But hold this Moment I have heard

The Tories, who of late appear'd,

Dejected, dull, and melancholy,

Are now once more grown brisk and jolly.

They've had the welcome News from *Spain*,

The Fleet's equipping out again ;

And Chevalier's to be Commander !

A weeping Chief ! great *Alexander*

Wept for more Worlds (as fays the Story,)

Merely for Fighting's Sake and Glory ,

But Chevalier in Peace delighting,

Wept for a Kingdom—not for Fighting !

I ne'er difturb my Head with Cares,

Of grand and weighty State-affairs ;

While *George* is *Britain*'s Faith's Defender,

I dread nor *Spaniard*, nor Pretender.

'Tis

'Tis Time, dear Coz, I now fhould ceafe,

And give us both a kind Releafe!

I'm fure I've tir'd myfelf, and you,

With this wild Rhapfody.　Adieu.

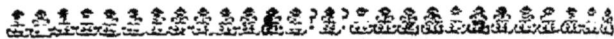

An Epiftle *to* Sir RICHARD STEELE;

On the Death of Mr Addifon.

IF I, O *Steele*ꞌ prefumptuous fhall appear,

And thefe unskilful Notes offend thy Ear,

Forbear to cenfure what I've artlefs writ,

No well-bred Man e'er damn'd a Woman's Wit.

But fure there's none of all th' infpir'd Train,

Who do not of thy Indolence complain !

Ingrate, or indolent ! or why, thus long,

Should *Addifon* require his Funeral-fong ?

When a lov'd Monarch quits his Cares below,

The meaneft Subjects join the common Woe,

But from the Fav'rite who his Worth beſt knew,

A Tribute of ſuperior Grief is due.

Shall *Ramſay*, and *Meliſſa* Lays produce,

That a Mechanick, this a Woman's Muſe.

While Thou, Wit's ſole ſurviving Hope, ſupine,

The melancholy Theme doſt ſtill decline ᵓ

Exert that Fire that glows within your Breaſt,

Nor longer thus in lazy Silence reſt;

Aloft your ſkilful Muſe can wing her Flight,

And emulate his Strains whoſe Praiſe you write.

For me, the meaneſt of the tuneful Train,

T' attempt th' unequal Task were fond and vain;

But could I ſing—Oh! ſacred Shade ꞌ thy Praiſe

Alone ſhould claim, alone inſpire my Lays.

Thou kind Preceptor of the tender Fair!

Great was the Charge, and generous the Care.

You ſhew'd us Virtue ſo celeſtial bright,

So amiable in ſo divine a Light;

Aſham'd

Afham'd at laft falfe Glories we refign'd,
By Thee inftructed to improve the Mind.

How oft reclin'd beneath a fylvan Shade,
Have I thy *Marcia* read, thy matchlefs Maid !
In her fuperior Worth, and Virtue fhine ;
Her Wifdom, Manners, her whole felf divine;
In her a great exalted Mind appears ;
And gentle *Lucia* melts my Soul to Tears.

Here, O ye Fair ! in this bright Mirror learn,
Your Minds with never-fading Charms t'adorn !
On thefe Accomplifhments beftow fome Care,
'Tis no great Merit, to be only fair.
His *Rofamonda* fhall for ever prove,
A Mark to keep us fafe from guilty Love.
Beauty's a Snare, unlefs with Virtue joyn'd,
An Angel-form, fhould have an Angel-mind;
But when the Bard difplays the artful Scene,
The fuppliant Beauty, and the vengeful Queen,

In melting Notes fings her difaft'rous Love ;
With Tears we pity what we can't approve.

How learn'd he was, O *Steele !* do thou declare ;
For that's a Task beyond a Woman's Sphere.
Some Works there are, wrought up by Rules of Art,
Where poor excluded Nature had no Part ;
But he the *Stagyrite*'s ftrict Axioms knew,
And ftill to Nature, as to Art was true.
He touch'd the Heart, the Paffions could command,
'Twas Nature all, but mended by his Hand.
Sublime his Style, his Sentiments refin'd,
Full of Benevolence to all Mankind.
In more than Theory he Religion knew,
And kept the Heav'nly Goddefs ftill in view ;
Rapt on her Wings, his Soul extatick foars,
Leaves our dull Orb, a better World explores,
And now he'as reach'd the Ethenal Plains above,
Th' eternal Seat of Harmony and Love ;

Bleft

Bleſt Harmony, and Love a-new inſpire,

With Hymns, like theirs, he joyns th' Angelick Quire.

He's gone! oh, never, never to return;

Around his Tomb, ye ſacred Muſes, mourn!

Your pious Tears on the cold Marble ſhed,

You lov'd him living, now lament him dead!

Cold is that Breaſt, where glow'd your hallow'd Fire,

Silent that Voice, whoſe Notes you did inſpire,

Still lies that Hand, the Lyre harmonious ſtrung,

Unmov'd the gen'rous Heart, and mute the tuneful

     Tongue!

That Dome, where his Remains now lye confin'd,

Holds not the Clay that held a nobler Mind.

Here peaceful reſt, to wait Heav'n's great Decree,

Soft be thy Slumbers, ſweet thy Waking be!

Who can his *Warwick*'s anxious Woes expreſs,

The bitter Anguiſh, and the deep Diſtreſs?

The lovely Mourner does not grieve alone ,

But diſtant *Cambria* echoes to each Groan;

Her native Country lends this poor Relief,

We weep, we ſigh, with ſimpathetick Grief.

Ev'n I, oppreſs'd with Sorrows of my own,

Suſpend them all to mourn her *Addiſon*.

O will She deign t' accept theſe lowly Lays,

My humble Muſe thus offers to his Praiſe!

O may the lovely Child, the budding Fair,

Sooth all her Griefs, and ſweeten every Care.

Still grow in Virtue, as ſhe grows in Years,

'Till ſhe in full-blown Excellence appears !

May ſhe be perfect, as his Fancy wrought,

" The Poet's Race excel the Poet's Thought !

Let blooming Charms united *Marcia* grace,

Her Sire's exalted Wit, her Mother's beauteous Face.

On

.

On reading the foregoing By THOMAS
GRIFFITH, *Efq*;

IN Lines fo foft you fpeak the Poet's Praife,
 Who wou'd not dye that cou'd infpire thy
  Lays!
And quit the gaudy Pleafures Life can give,
In fweet *Meliffa's* deathlefs Verfe to live;
E'en much lov'd *Addifon* we lefs lament,
Since thou haft rais'd him fuch a Monument!
So well the Poet, and the Chriftian's drawn,
As muft excel all Features, but thy own.

A

A THOUGHT,

Occasioned by being present at the Death of a Friend ;
May 28, 1720.

HOW dreadful 'tis to yield this fleeting Breath!
Well art thou stil'd the King of Terrors,
Death !

If ought could reconcile us to thy Sway,

And make the Soul content to leave its Clay;

Here might we learn.—How peaceful she resigns,

Her Faith still rising, as her Strength declines!

With fervent Longings she desires to be

From this frail, sinful Tabernacle free,

O dear Redeemer, and to rest with Thee !

Her Pray'rs are heard ,—the pious Soul is fled '

Oh ' may we all that now lament the Dead,

Prepare to meet our own approaching Dooms '

Unknown the Hour, at which the Master comes

Here

Here uninform'd we fee the mortal Frame;
The Soul's return'd to Heav'n from whence it came,
This Body fhall in Time rife up again,
And re-united with the Soul remain;
This Tongue now mute, in Hymns employ'd fhall be,
And thefe dark Eyes their Maker's Face fhall fee.

How fweet is the Rememb'rance of the juft!
It flourifhes in Death, and bloffoms in the Duft.
To me thy Mem'ry fhall be ever dear,
God's gracious Work did in thy Life appear ;
May his renewing Grace my Soul refine,
And grant my latter End may be like thine !

✛✛✛✛✛✛✛✛✛✛✛✛✛✛✛✛✛ ✛✛✛✛✛✛✛✛✛✛✛✛✛✛✛✛✛

On a Sight of the foregoing Lines. By N.
GRIFFITHS, *Efq;*

THUS human Wit is truly made divine,

When Heaven itfelf infpires a Soul like

thine '

Thus ever write ! devoutly thus afpire

To join, before thy Time, the bleft celeftial Choii '

We too in thy Applaufe will learn to foar,

Forget *Meliffa*, and the Saint adore.

HYMN *to the* CREATOR.

I.

O Wife Creator, Pow'r immenfe,

Who built this wond'rous Flame !

Thy Wifdom and Omnipotence,

Thy glorious Works proclaim.

The

II.

The unfashion'd Mass thy Wisdom made
   In beauteous Order shine;
And all the spacious Void obey'd
   Thy forming Pow'r divine.

III.

These pois'd the Earth, and fix'd each Pole,
   And bade the Ocean flow;
The radiant Orbs, and Stars that roll,
   To Thee their Lustre owe.

IV.

O how stupendous is thy Pow'r,
   How fathomless thy Ways'
No human Wit can them explore,
   They mock our weak Essays.

V.

O how astonishing thy Love,
   Thy Mercy and thy Truth '
How gently, Lord, dost thou reprove
   Th' Offences of my Youth!

In

VI.

In Folly I've confum'd my Time,
    And Error's wand'ring Maze ;
Forgive, O Lord ! my former Crime,
    And guard my future Days.

VII.

My Mind, like the firft formlefs Wafte,
    Is void of Light and Grace ;
Confus'd Ideas jarring hafte,
    O'er all the gloomy Space.

VIII.

Let thy enlight'ning Beams appear,
    Reform my froward Will ;
My Reafon let thy Wifdom clear,
    Thy Love my Spirit fill.

IX.

My vain Defires, O Lord controul,
    Renewing Grace beftow !
Lift up my dull and ftupid Soul
    From Grov'ling here below.

My

X.

My lifeleſs, cold, corrupted Mind,
    With holy Ardour fire;
That when 'tis from the Droſs refin'd,
    To Thee it may aſpire.

XI.

To Thee, Almighty Pow'r ſupreme,
    In grateful Songs I'd ſoar'
And ſtill perſue th' eternal Theme,
    Eternally adore

EPISTLE *to Mr* THO. GRIFFITH, 1720.

INGENIOUS Youth, who ſtudiouſly prepare
    To make the Health of human Kind your Care,
To You, I now endite, in penſive Strain,
Who late addreſs'd you in a jocund Vein.

If there be ought within the Pow'r of Art,
Of Force to cure a Sorrow-wounded Heart,

To mitigate the Torments of the Mind,
And from oppreſſive Woes relieve Mankind,
Oh ! find the Secret in its dark Receſs,
And ſighing Millions will thy Labours bleſs !

But oh ! how vain it is to hope Relief
From Phyſick's Art for Love or anxious Grief!
The Torments of the firſt, you beſt can tell,
And I, the Anguiſh of the laſt too well.
But ſuch dire Ills, which will admit no Cure,
Kind Heav'n enables Mortals to endure;
And for Diſeaſes whoſe Malignance kill,
Allows us to employ the learn'd Phyſician's Skill.
Let ſuch, O *Griffith* ! thy Preceptors be,
Let ſuch engage thy ſtudious Scrutiny;
From their *Arcana* cull the choiceſt Store,
And Nature's wond'rous Myſteries explore.

Phœbus, the God of Phyſick, and of Wit,
To *Daphne*'s Beauty did his Pow'r ſubmit;

His

His Skill in Herbs, and on the *Golden Lyre*,

Affords no Cure for Love's relentlefs Fire.

To charm the Nymph harmonious Lays he tries,

He eagerly perfues, fhe coyly flies;

Dubious the Strife did for a while appear ;

The God was wing'd by Love, the Nymph by Fear.

But Love prevails; he fprings to catch the Fair,

When *Peneus* fhe invokes, who hears her Pray'r.

She's turn'd to Laurel in th' unequal Chace,

And thus transform'd eludes the God's Embrace.

Phœbus, thus mock'd, did in his Wrath ordain,

That all who fing like him, like him fhould meet

      Difdain

But yet to eafe Defpair, he did decree

The fweet condoling Charms of Poetry ;

And to his genuine favour'd Sons allows

A Wreath of Laurel to adorn their Brows.

Like *Phœbus*, Thou haft lov'd, like *Phœbus*, fung

Harmonious Lays ftill flowing from thy Tongue;

The Malediction too thy Youth has born,

In haughty *Sachariſſa's* cruel Scorn.

For Love diſdain'd, accept of unſought Praiſe;

Phœbus himſelf preſents Thee with the Bays!

Wou'd he propitious to my Wiſh attend,

A nobler Gift ſhould recompenſe my Friend;

Such as on *Æſculapius* he beſtow'd,

To whom the Science he reveal'd and ſhew'd :

The Son did in his Father's Arts ſucceed,

And, from contagious Ills, the *Latians* free'd.

May Heav'n, from *Britain*, ſuch dire Plagues avert,

And guard us from the peſtilential Dart !

To ſuff'ring Neighbours ſmiling Health reſtore,

And keep th' impending Danger from our Shore!

The wond'rous Faculty employs your Mind,

You ſtudy to be uſeful to Mankind,

O may th' All-wiſe propitiouſly incline,

The true *Apollo* bleſs thy great Deſign !

Gracious

Gracious to Thee, his Supplicant, impart

Myfterious Secrets of the healing Art!

May'ft thou in Riches, and in Honours fhare,

And future Kings be trufted to thy Care :

And may'ft thou be (kind Heav'n the Wifh allow,)

As learn'd, as much rever'd, as *Mead* is now.

A QUERY. *Occafioned by Reading*
PRIOR'*s Alma* .

To One that loves good Eating.

Written at the Requeft of Sir R. M.

FOR ever bleft be *Prior*'s Shade !
Such Demonftration he has made,

Of *Alma*'s Progrefs thro' all Ages,

And eke of all her different Stages ;

That Whimfeys of the Pineal-Gland

(Which few, or none, can underftand)

Are to my Thinking now become,

Like Tales of *Long Meg*, or *Tom Thumb*.

—But

—But what, says *Thomas*, means this Rapture ?
Be pleas'd to read quite thro' the Chapter;
And then perhaps you'll take the Hint:
—I mean, if there be any in't.

    That *Alma*'s Bent, or Inclination,
Is influenc'd by her Situation:
If her Abode be fresh and gay,
Her Bias is to sportive Play ;
But if her Lodging is grown crazy,
She's, or too careful, or too lazy.
Two Instances I will apply,
Which you will grant, or else deny.
Sure, as you hate a long Epistle,
Young *Charlotte*'s Maid still hunts the Whistle ;
While *Jane* by adverse Fate made dull,
And just but one Degree 'bove Fool,
Is frugal, as Friend *Christian* thought,
  [1] anxious how to save the Groat.

                             When

When *Orpheus* touches his Bass-viol,

(These Truths admit of no Denial.)

Soon as th' harmonious Sounds we hear,

Alma is charm'd up to the Ear ;

When we partake the rich Repast,

Then *Alma* dwells upon the Taste ;

From whence some would draw Inferences,

That *Alma*'s self is but the Senses.

To your wise Sex we yield Dominion;

Pray, send us your profound Opinion,

If when the Bacon eats delicious,

Or brisk *Champaign* drinks rich and luscious,

Resolve my Doubt, and plainly tell me,

Is *Alma*, in the Taste, or Belly ?

QUERINDA

To J-------N M----------R *Esq*;

OPPRESS'D with Ills, and funk beneath the
      Weight

Of anxious Grief, and unrelenting Fate,

Succeffive Woes, and never-ceafing Care,

Abandon'd to Misfortune and Defpair,

How can the gloomy long neglected Mufe

One tuneful Strain, or cheerful Thought infufe ?

—But elevated Worth, like *Phœbus'* Rays,

E'en thro' the Gloom, *its* Influence difplays;

Sufpends my Griefs, infpires with Joy fupreme,

Pleafure immenfe, while *M—ll—r* is my Theme !

With each fuperior Excellence replete,

Virtue innate, and Soul fublimely great,

The Subftitute of Heav'n you feem to ftand,

Beftowing Plenty with a bounteous Hand.

M   The

The beſt of Brothers, and the beſt Ally !

Thrice happy they who on your Care rely !

Secure of all that may their Wiſhes pleaſe,

Splendor, Indulgence, Affluence, and Eaſe.

May thoſe whom you with Love inceſſant bleſs,

Revere your Goodneſs, and your Worth confeſs !

How noble, how benevolent, you are,

Let Obligation ſpeak, and Gratitude declare ;

Shou'd thoſe be mute,—-yet Truth will force its
     Way,

And blaze your Merit in the Face of Day.

With Wiſdom, Honour, Wealth, you're amply
     bleſs'd,

Three Talents rarely by one Man poſſeſs'd ;

But, Sir, your Chriſtian Graces far excel,

Rich in good Works, and wiſe in living well .

True Wiſdom you have found, celeſtial Grace !

Her Ways are pleaſant, and her Paths are Peace.

In this uncommon Path ſtill perſevere,

And of the pious Few ſtill Chief appear,

May that kind Pow'r who all your Good conveys,

Crown you with Health, Content, and Length of

    Days '

The choiceſt Talents have too much Allay,

Till bright Religion's pure refining Ray

With beatifick Graces makes them ſhine,

And her Impreſſion ſtamps them all divine.

Ev'n Wiſdom is too frequently auſtere,

And over-awes with Look and Brow ſevere,

Learning, and Knowledge, (valu'd Gifts ') may be

To Oſtentation prone, and Self-ſufficiency,

Riches, and Honour, too, too oft miſguide,

And prompt the Soul to Avarice, or Pride.

But where Religion is, her Pow'r is ſeen,

The Wiſe inſtructs with Countenance ſerene

The

The Learn'd convinc'd that Nothing's all he knows,

Looks to the Source, whence perfect Knowledge

    flows

The Rich is liberal, humble is the Great,

And condescends to those of low Estate.

  One of these Gifts by such is oft possest,

Who want, or want a Relish for, the Rest;

A Talent this, a Virtue that does crown,

Accumulated Gifts are rarely known ;

But left for ever we despair to find

All these Endearments in one Man combin'd,

Propitious Heav'n has join'd them once, we see,

Ad gen'rous *M—ll—r* is the wond'rous He.

Written

Written in Mr LAW's *Treatise on Chri-
ʃtian Perfection ; being the Gift of
Mrs* MYDDELTON.

CHRISTIAN Perfection with more Luftre
      fhines,

In the bright Giver's Life, than Author's Lines;

His rigid Senfe, the Cynick much betrays,

Her heavenly Life, the perfect Soul difplays ;

With each accomplifh'd Grace, in her are joyn'd

The Chriftian Frame, and Sanctity of Mind.

The one Thing needful wifely is her Care ,

Too few alas ! of fuch Examples are !

Thofe num'rous Virtues rarely meet in one,

Which we admire, in matchlefs *Myddelton.*

To Mrs MARY HALE; Jan. 1, 1728.
With Mr WAL-LER's *Poems.*

I.

NOW *Janus* turns his youthful Face,
    The common Wiſh no doubt you hear,
Which flows from ev'ry Mouth apace,
    I wiſh you, Mad'm, a happy Year.

II

But you, whom Heav'n indulgent plac'd
    Beneath its lov'd *Maria's* Care,
Maria, with each Virtue grac'd,
    That e'er adorn'd the Wife, or Fair.

III.

Maria, whoſe exalted Senſe,
    With ſtricteſt Piety is joyn'd,
And each ſuperior Excellence,
    With the moſt humble Chriſtian Mind.

You

IV

You, who such Happiness enjoy,

 Can no new Wish expect from me,

Nor can I frame one Thought of Joy,

 Could add to your Felicity

V.

May you continue still her Care,

 In Health and Happiness sincere;

And long may Heav'n *Maria* spare,

 Long bless us with one Angel here'

VI.

My Numbers harsh and incorrect,

 A Taste so delicate can't please;

But sure, great *Waller* you'll respect,

 The Bard so fam'd for tuneful Lays'

VII.

He, your Acceptance humbly craves,

 Ambitious to preserve his Fame,

And begs you would adorn his Leaves,

 With the Inscription of your Name.

On

●❈●❈●❈'●❈●❈●❈●❈'●❈●❈●❈●❈'●❈●❈●

On *Mrs* MYDDELTON's *Picture :*

Drawn by Mr HOLLAND.

O' Had I *Holland*'s wond'rous Art to trace
　　Th' engaging Sweetnefs of the lovely Face!
Or, Words divine as *Addifon*'s could find
T' exprefs th' Heav'nly Beauties of the Mind!
Inceffant fhould my Pen, and Pencil, be
Delightfully employ'd, O *Myddelton*! on Thee'

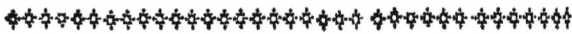

❖❖❖❖❖❖❖❖❖❖❖❖❖❖❖❖❖❖❖❖ ❖❖❖❖❖ ❖❖❖❖❖❖

To the Author of the Progrefs *of* Poetry,

Printed in the White-Hall *Evening* Poft.

HAIL, O tenth Mufe' nor fcorn the artlefs
　　Praife,
One of thy Sex to thy fmooth Numbers pays,

Thy

Thy mighty Genius in diftinguifh'd Light,

Soft-flowing, copious, active, ftrong and bright,

Artful difplays a laurel'd facred Train,

In fo fublime, fo heav'nly fweet a Strain,

The moft harmonious of th' harmonious Choir,

Or *Phœbus* felf might yield to Thee his Lyre.

To Mrs MARY HALE ; Jan 1, 1729.

With PRIOR's *Poems.*

GAY *Prior*, fam'd for jocund Song,
Lov'd to amufe the Fair and Young ,

Then wonder not, his Lays appear

To wifh my Friend a happy Year

May Health reftor'd, a Mind at Eafe,

Refrefhing Nights, and cheaiful Days,

Be ever thine , and Joys ftill run,

Inceffant as the circling Sun '

May'ft

May'ft thou, (ye Pow'rs regard my Pray'r ')

Be ftill *Maria's* tender Care !

Kind Heav'n did well for thee provide ,

A Saint is both thy Guard, and Guide

 O D E . *On the Birth-day of the Ho nour'd Mrs* MYDDELTON. Feb. 8

I.

ARISE, fair Sun ' profufely gay,
 In all thy radiant Glories dreft,
All thy refplendent Locks difplay,
 Shine forth as in thy native Eaft.
To our cold North thy Pow'r extend,
 And kindly Warmth convey;
Thy choiceft Beams, and Bleffings fend,
 To crown this happy Day '

II. Hail

II.

Hafte from the Wint'ry Signs, and chafe
  Bleak Winds, keen Froft, and Sleets from hence;
Roll on thy Orb a quicker Pace,
  Here, fhed thy vernal Influence
Awake the Flow'rs, and Bloffoms gay,
  Let *Zephir* Odours bring ,
May this diftinguifh'd Natal Day
  Anticipate the Spring !

III.

Hail Day ' when Heav'n, propitious kind,
  To *Cambria* gave a matchlefs Dame,
Whofe graceful Form, and God-like Mind,
  Ev'n daring Atheifts might reclaim.
With ev'ry Grace profufely blefs'd,
  With ev'ry Charm replete ,
In her fair Virtue ftands confefs'd,
  And fmiles ferenely Great.

IV. Perception

IV.

Perception clear, a Genius fine,
　　With Elegance of Tafte unite;
Religion, Learning, Wifdom, joyn
　　To form her Soul divinely bright.
Her Bounty, Charity, Good-will,
　　Do evidently fhew,
The focial Train her Bofom fill,
　　And thence inceffant flow.

V.

But oh! how vain the giddy Mufe,
　　That for unequal lowly Lays,
Dares an exalted Subject chufe,
　　And offer difproportion'd Praife!
Affift your Sex, ye tuneful Nine,
　　Attend the darling Theme,
Let Numbers, Senfe, and Fancy fhine
　　Bright as *Maria*'s Fame !

VI.

How vain th' Attempt ! *Erato* cries,

   Can'ft thou e'er count the fhining Train

Of glitt'ring Stars, that croud the Skies?

   The bearded Product of the Plain ?

The Leaves which Autumn's Tempefts fell?

   The liquid Pearls that deck the Morn?

Then, count the Charms, the Graces tell,

   That lovely *Myddelton* adorn!

✿✿✿✿✿✿✿✿✿✿✿✿ ✿✿✿✿✿✿✿✿✿ ✿✿✿✿

To Mrs MARY BENNET, *who defired me to write out the Mottos, and Decorations of Sir* RICHARD TREVOR'S *Pictures ; in the Gallery at* Trevalyn.

TIR'D with Quadrille, th' Affembly Room
      I fled,

And left the Living to behold the Dead;

In

In penfive Mood the Gallery I fought,
And there indulg'd a melancholy Thought.

Here, Canvas *Cæfars* fternly guard the Wall,
As monft'rous as the Giants in *Guild-Hall*,
There *Villiers*, *Deza* here, the Painter drew,
Sure, *Vandyke*'s Art we in thofe Pieces view'
From Works of unskill'd Hands I turn my Sight,
Hands, as unfit to paint, as —mine to write.
Here, *Rome*'s fworn En'my, who, in *Cannæ*'s Field,
Taught the World's Conqu'rors to his Arms to yield,
And there, great *Charles*, who with fuperior Mind,
Th' Empire, *Indies*, and the World, refign'd.
Here, flaught'ring Chiefs who Terror us'd to move,
And there, fair Ladies who infpir'd with Love.
—Concern'd the fading Copies I furvey'd,
—Alas! th' Originals are quite decay'd,
Death o'er their Triumphs did his own advance,
And forc'd his Captives to learn *Holben*'s Dance.

None Living now are reprefented heie,

Thofe fleep in Death, who in thefe Shades appear.

A folemn Scene ! where ev'ry thoughtful Mind

May, in each Piece, *Memento mori* find.

In Contemplation loft,—at laft I view

Your fav'rite Knight, then Madam, think of you;

The Thoughts of you can always Pleafure give,

They've charm'd me from the Dead,—I find I live !

I run for Pen and Ink, and with Delight

Write down the Trophies of the youthful Knight;

Cordials, Conferves, with which, when grown a Sage,

He cheer'd his Heart in his declining Age.

Could I his Picture draw, I'd fend that too;

Were he alive, I might have more to do,

Perhaps, his Secretary I fhould be,

To write his Thanks in high-flown Poetry.

The courtly Knight, no doubt, would think it
     meet

To lay his Puns, and Picture at your Feet.

And

And to'ards a new Collection club his Song,

And rival *Corbet*, and gay *Lashington*,

Nay, what (I doubt) would make myself repine,

He'd out-do *Howard*'s finish'd Verse,—and Mine.

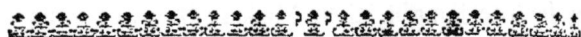

On Mrs SYBIL EGERTON's *singing an Anthem in* Wrexham *Church*, June 21, 1730.

IN *Maro*'s Fiction, the *Cumean* Maid
Conducts *Æneas* to the *Elizian* Shade,

The *Sybil*'s pow'rful Call soon gains Access,

To their imagin'd Realms of Harmony and Bliss.

What Thanks do we our real *Sybil* owe,

For giving us a Taste of Heav'n, below?

No gloomy Paths, or Caves, for her we trod,

She shone an Angel in the House of God.

When to her Maker's Praise, she tunes her Voice,

What Soul's not rapt, what Heart does not rejoyce!

She

She, on the Royal Poet's Words beſtows,

Such moving Airs, as he did erſt compoſe,

When to his God he ſtrung the living Lyre,

And *Sion*'s Daughters joyn'd th' harmonious Choir.

While her celeſtial Strains our Ears invade,

Methinks, I ſee the venerable * Shade,

Charm'd with the Notes ſhe ſo divinely ſings,

Strive to awake his Harp, and animate the Strings.

Sure, Angels joy'd to hear their Heav'nly Song,

In Heav'nly Strains, flow from a mortal Tongue !

Bleſt Maid ! to God thy tuneful Voice devote,

Let *Allelija*'s ever grace thy each melodious Note.

* King *David*'s Picture.

✦✦✦✦✦✦✦✦✦✦✦✦✦✦✦✦✦✦✦✦✦✦✦✦✦✦✦✦✦✦✦✦✦

To S. Y------KE, *Esq*;

Occasioned by Mr W—ld's *Verses to him in Praise of the foregoing.*

YOUR Friend's kind Applause is so clever and
      clean,
I fear in my Heart it will make me grow vain;
Tho' Flattery is what you Men make a Jest on,
Yet 'tis what we Women too greedily feast on.
Ambrosia, or *Nectar,* had ne'er such a Flavour:
Who offers this Incense, *sans* doubt, wins our Favour.
This granted; th' Effect of Course is allow'd,
Which is, that it makes us fantastick and proud.
Should this be my Case—should I grow pert and
      bold!
Why, Sir, you must thank your good Friend *Wy-*
      mondsold,
Who so with his Praise has cajol'd me of late,
That my Brain, like a Whirligigg, turns in my Pate.
                      You

You cunningly bribe me with Compliments terfe,

To furnifh you ftill with fome more of my Verfe;

When they've coft you a Reading, when you've found ev'ry Fault,

Tho' they are not far-fetch'd, you'll think them dear bought.

For, in my own Judgment, there's nothing that mine is,

But flags long before you can reach near a Finis.

You ask ftill for more ; fhould I bring a whole Book,

And add Annotations ' how fimply you'd look !

Suppofe that *Meliffa* to you fhould demean, as

Once to the Author of *Qui fit Mecænas*—

Did th' impertinent Scribbler, who'd pafs for a Wit?

—He talk'd your Friend *Horace* into fplenetick Fit.

Should

Should I ferve you fo; pray, who can you blame,

But *T—ke*, and his merry Friend *M—tt* for the fame?

—I'll reprieve you this Time, if you'll but recommend

My Service and Thanks to your complaifant Friend,

And believe that I am, without the leaft Grumble,

In Verfe, or plain Profe,

     Tour Servant moft Humble.

To Mrs ROBERTS *on her Spinning.*

Written on her Birth-day, Jan. 6, 1731.

PENELOPE did thus her Time employ,

 Till her lov'd wand'ring Lord return'd from
  Troy;

While He was fated thro' ftrange Realms to roam,

The prudent Queen play'd the good Wife at Home;

While he the various Turns of Fortune knew,

She ply'd the Loom, and th' Ivory Shuttle threw.

So the dull Hours you at your Wheel deceive,
And draw a Web, fit for a Queen to weave.

Wife the Refolve, when to your Wheel you fate,
The Wheel, beft Emblem of our worldly State;
Still changing, varying, always moving found,
Where high and low, alternate, take their round,
With skilful Hand you manage this Machine,
May like Succefs thro' all your Life be feen !
May each revolving Year with Joy be crown'd,
And this your Natal Day ftill happy found !

Let no proud Dame the Spinning Art defpife,
Which from the wife *Minerva* took its Rife ;
And which *Aliza* for Amufement chofe
To lighten Abfence, and to foften Woes.

To the Honourable Miſs STEWART, *now Counteſs of* Seaforth, *on the Death of her Brother, the Honourable* ALEXAN-DER STEWART, *Eſq*;

SAY, Mourner, ſay ! can nought thy Spirits cheer ?

Wilt thou no more the Voice of Comfort hear !

Still muſt that tender Boſom throb with Woe ?

Still muſt thoſe radiant Eyes with Tears o'erflow ?

Still wilt thou droop, like ſome Fair fading Flow'r'

Shall canker Grief thy roſy Bloom devour ?

Or, can a friendly ſympathizing Heart,

That in thy Weight of Sorrow bears a Part,

That feels thy Anguiſh, and repeats thy Sighs,

Bleeds for each Tear that floods thy beauteous Eyes,

Say ! can this Heart, that makes thy Suff'rings mine,

Dear lovely Mourner ! give ſome Eaſe to thine ?

How

How great thy Lofs, how juft thy Sorrows are,
All thofe who knew the noble Youth declare:
'Tis own'd, that rarely Worth like his appears,
Mature in Wifdom in the Bloom of Years :
And Virtue, fure, by Wifdom's underftood ;
For none are truly wife, but who are good.

Each focial Grace, with Piety combin'd,
To form in *Stewart* the moft perfect Mind :
Science he lov'd, and could in Arts excel,
But chofe th' important Part of living well.
While in his Profpect all could Life adorn,
With Honours waiting for the nobly born ,
By all carefs'd, refpected and approv'd,
By her he lov'd the moft, the moft belov'd ;
While round his Heart the lambent Paffions play'd,
He, the dread Summons reverenc'd, and obey'd,
Ere yet four *Luftra* o'er his Head were paft,
The Shades of Death his Morn of Life o'ercaft .

Cut

Cut down, in his gay Spring, and sweetest Bloom;
So Flow'rs are gather'd to adorn a Tomb.

But tell me, thou! whom *Stewart* lov'd the most,
In losing Life, what has thy Brother lost?
Has he lost Honours ?—Could those Honours vie
With all the Glories he partakes on high?
Who would not lay a fading Garland down,
When summon'd to receive a starry Crown?
The best Society that Mortals boast,
Who would not quit, to join th' Angelic Host?
How poor th' imperfect Bliss this World can lend,
To those full Pleasures which can never end '

Repine not, that his Race was run so soon;
He reach'd the Goal before Life's scorching Noon,
When the wild Passions rage, and Reason's Force
Can scarce retain them within Virtue's Course :
Since none too soon can reach the blest Abode,
Who would dislike the Shortness of the Road?

Cease

Ceaſe then thy fruitleſs Sighs, fair Mourner,
　　ceaſe !

And to thy gentle Heart reſtore its Peace :

All due Regard to Nature has been ſhewn,

Let Reaſon now reſume its wonted Throne,

Let Comfort's cheering Ray diſpel the Gloom,

That Cloud of Sorrow which obſcures thy Bloom :

The pious Youth has thoſe bleſt Realms explor'd,

Where on Devotion's Wings he oft had ſoar'd.

He's gone,——where late, oh ! late, may'ſt thou
　　appear !

Heav'n ſpare thee long, a bright Example here !

On the Death of Mrs MARY BENNET.

Printed in the Magazine for March 1735.

IN Silence ftill muft I the Lofs lament,
    Nor give, o'er-charg'd, my fwelling Sorrows Vent?
Muft ftill the anxious Sigh, the fwelling Tear,
Be all the Vouchers that my Grief's fincere ?
Can I Relief in fad Reflection find,
While her dear Image fills my penfive Mind.
Or, can my Thoughts, when taught in Verfe to flow,
Exprefs her Worth, or mitigate my Woe ?

  My Mind prefents her, as fhe did appear,
When well fhe pafs'd her fhort Probation here,
And warmly practis'd ev'ry Heav'nly Grace,
To prove a Conqueror in the Chriftian Race.
Methinks, I fee her—as fhe late was feen,
Humble, and free, obliging and ferene,

Methinks, I hear Her, and with Joy attend

To the sweet Converse of th' instructive Friend,

In whose pure Soul each hallow'd Virtue glow'd,

As radiant Stars emblaze the milky Road.

Whose soft Compassion, simpathizing Care,

Extensive spread, and unconfin'd as Air.

Whose Manners winning, easy and refin'd,

The sure Result of an accomplish'd Mind

Tho' polish'd, yet not varnish'd with one Wile,

An *Israelite*! in whom there was no Guile.

When I, dear Saint ! do not thy Loss deplore,

And on thy well-spent Life reflect no more;

When thy Memorial is no longer dear,

Or, I thy honour'd Name no more revere.

When I forget thy Virtues; may I be,

Forgot by those, who most resemble Thee.

To

To a LADY. *On her* Marriage.

WHILE the unthinking *Fair* with Paſſion doat
On the gay *Plume*, or military *Coat*;
While the fond Heart, or giddy Fancy's ſmit
With flaught'ring *Chief*, or the more flaught'ring Wit.
You, Madam! ſway'd by Reaſon's ſacred Voice,
Make the humane Philoſopher your Choice;
Wiſely beſtowing on the Man of Truth
The Charms of Beauty, Innocence, and Youth.

Virtue with Temper, Wit with Candour join'd,
Honour, that flows from Rectitude of Mind;
The Head judicious, Heart ſincere and true,
Diſtinguiſh HIM, whom Heav'n reſerv'd for you.

The

The Royal *Sage*, unrival'd in Renown,
Whofe Wifdom fhone far brighter than his Crown,
Has more than once this certain Judgment giv'n—
" A prudent Wife's the Gift of bounteous Heav'n.
The Heav'nly Gift your Spoufe receives with Pride,
Views the good Wife, in the dear blooming Bride.
While you, with Pleafure, may his Worth regard,
And fign this Maxim of our famous Bard—
" A Wit's a Feather, and a Chief's a Rod,
" An honeft Man's the nobleft Work of God."

Your Prudence, in your well-judg'd Option's
    fhewn;
Rewarding Merit, you enhance your own.
That Union, fure! compleatly bleft muft piove,
Founded on Virtue, juft Efteem, and Love!
Happy, thrice Happy! may ye be through Life!
He the beft Husband, you the kindeft Wife!

Accept

Accept thefe Gratulations, void of Art;

My Hand tranfcribes the Language of my Heart.

Nor wait I for *Apollo*'s tuneful Aid,

Or Infpiration of *Pierian* Maid,

Nor *Hymen* call, to blefs the nuptial Day,

But ardent Wifhes, in few Words, convey.

Soft, light, and eafy be the Marriage Yoke!

May the next Cent'ry fee the Chain unbroke !

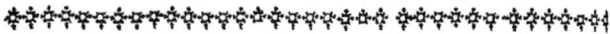

O N

Mrs MYDDELTON's *Birth-day*, Feb. 8.

Tune, Tweed-Side.

I.

YE Mufes, and Graces appear,
 Unite all your Skill, and advance ;

With Mufick, thofe ravifh the Ear,

 Thefe, gracefully move in the Dance.

Grief

Grief here no Admittance fhall find ;

  Let our Joy be fincere and ferene ;

Sincere, as *Maria*'s bright Mind,

  Obliging, and free, as her Mien.

II.

Let the Harp all its Harmony lend,

  With Mufick enliven each String;

Let the Voice in fweet Warblings afcend,

  While *Maria*, *Maria*! we fing:

Bleft Harmony dwells on her Tongue,

  Oh! 'tis Heav'n, when Silence fhe breaks!

Not the Spheres cou'd excell our fweet Song,

  Cou'd we fing, with the Grace, that fhe fpeaks.

To Mrs MYDDELTON, *on the Death of her*
Canary Bird, who dy'd on her Birth
day, Feb. 8. *The same Day a Gentleman*
had sent a Copy of Verses on the Bird.

HOW fleet our Joys! how subject to Decay!
 The Muse, who jocund sung your natal

  Day,

Now flaggs the Wings, and droops the languid

  Head,

And mourns, with gen'rous Grief, a Rival dead;

A happy Rival, whose melodious Strain

Cou'd soften Sorrow, and alleviate Pain.

While I, alas! with Words attempt to please,

Words that want Pow'r, or Pain, or Grief, to ease.

 O sweetest Chaunter of the feather'd Choir!

Far thy harmonious Pipe excell'd my Lyre.

No more, ah me! thy Melody we hear,
No more thy Warblings charm *Maria*'s Ear.
Penfive, alas! in her now filent Room,
She mourns thy fudden, unexpected Doom.

Did the fweet Harp, and * *Babby*'s tuneful Throat,
To jealous Emulation fwell thy Note ?
Did'ft thou, poor Bird! beyond thy Strength effay,
And, in the Conteft, fing thy Soul away !

O fweet Mufician ! whither art thou fled,
In the blefs'd Shades feek'ft thou thy Kindred dead?
Where in a Grove, amidft the warbling Throng,
With *Strada*'s Nightingale thou joyn'ft in Song.
O may'ft thou Sounds articulate attain,
And chaunt *Maria*, thro' th' *Elizian* Plain '

If deathlefs Fame my artlefs Verfe cou'd give,
Like *Lesbia*'s Sparrow's, thy lov'd Name fhou'd live.

Q   —How

* A young Lady that fing there

—How vain the Thought !—as if Fame could be-
    ftow

Honours more great, than what thou here did'ft
    know ?

Did not thy Miftrefs feed thee Day by Day ?

And live not thy fweet Notes in *Orpheus'* Lay ?

Thy Glory to the higheft Pitch was rais'd,

Lov'd by *Maria*, and by *Orpheus* prais'd.

By a Gentleman, on feeing the forego-ing Verfes.

TH' unknown *Meliffa* may be gay,
    And blooming as the Month of *May*,
Frefh as *Aurora's* Eaftern Rays,
And wake a World to fing her Praife;
But Weftern Rays appear decay'd,
And Bloffoms fall, and Colours fade,
A Hint, *Meliffa*! if a Maid.

Or like *Apollo's Zenith* Hour;

Or like a full blown Rose its Pow'r,

Paſt Bud and balmy Honey-dew

Unfolds, and ſet her Seed in View,

Moſt ſweetly deck'd in Golden Hue ,

Or like autmnal, plenteous Horn !

With ripen'd Fruits and Sheaves of Corn;

Indulgent to the World ſhe yields

The Produce of her cultur'd Fields.

Or if the frigid Seaſon's nigh,

Life's Winter Cold benumb'd and dry,

I value not the outward Form,

The beauteous Soul is young and warm.

Then let *Meliſſa's* Age be Morn,

Or Noon, or Eve, or Night forlorn;

Or let her outward Form be grac'd

With ev'ry Beauty juſtly plac'd.

Or deck'd with every lying Sign

That all within is not divine ;

Her Numbers, Humour, Force, and Fire,

My Soul enraptur'd muft admire.

W. C.

❀❀❀❀❀❀|❀❀❀❀❀❀❀❀|❀❀❀❀❀❀❀❀|❀❀❀❀❀❀

To Mrs MYDDELTON ; February 16.
By G. SH----R----Y, *Efq*;

*A*MANDA commands me to write,

   Who have neither Genius, nor Art,

Never faw *Parnaffus*'s Height,

   And hate its cold Springs from my Heart.

What can I then do ? I muft chufe

   Kefu-Tcha, or fome fuch high Hill ;

She herfelf muft act as the Mufe

   To inform, and govern my Quill.

I'll

I'll try then. O Heavenly Maid!
   " Adored *Amanda* !"—what's next?
Nay, you muft not refufe me your Aid,
   Since I have chofe you for my Text.

Your Text? Quoth Mifs *Hale* who ftood by,
   So bafhful! yet now grown fo pert!
I fear it is *Sapho*, and I,
   Have made you fo very alert.

She thought you like *Orpheus* could play,
   And your Tunes have fav'd our dear Bird ;
I'm fure ne'er a Tree danc'd that Day,
   And *Canny* has never fince ftir'd.

I too in the Snare was foon caught,
   And civilly joyn'd with the Reft
The Fiddler to thank, whom we thought
   Endeavour'd to fiddle his Beft.

                           But

But tho' of a Bird you may sing,

 And chirp out some little low Lay,

Exceed not the Strength of your String,

 Nor on loftier Subjects essay.

Call * *Sancho* faithful, *Fiddy* lame,

 Perhaps with such Themes you may cope;

Prophane not my *Amanda*'s Name,

 But leave it to *Swift*, or to *Pope*.

    * Favourite Dogs.

To Miss HALE, *on seeing the foregoing.* Feb. 19.

OF the sage God *Apollo* full oft have I read,

 And oft his quaint Sayings have ran in my

Head;

        I've

I've conn'd all his Titles, and Offices o'er ;

Yet of me the leaft Notice he ne'er took before.

Mifguided by old fafhion'd Poets, I thought,

At *Delos*, or *Delphos*, he ftill muft be fought ;

Or on Top of *Parnaffus*, cajoling the Mufes ,—

—But the ftrolling God, a new Refidence chufes.'

No wonder, that I cou'd ne'er find him at Home,

Since he has remov'd both himfelf and his Dome !

But who could imagine, his Godfhip wou'd make

A Tour to our Hills, and *Parnaffus* forfake !

For thus it is whifper'd—(if true be the Tale,)

He fpeaks at *Kefn-Tcha*, his Prieftefs Mifs *Hale*.

But tell me, dear Prieftefs, O tell me the Truth !

Were not the laft Words that he put in your Mouth,

A genteel Reprimand to her who effay'd

To fing our *Maria* without Art, or his Aid ?

Muft none, to fucceed on that Subject, e'er hope,

If they can't fing as well, as a *Swift*, or a *Pope* ?

But did he not add, (if the Truth you wou'd tell,)
That his genuine Son *Sh——y* fings full as well?

'Tis fomewhere recorded, and you, and I know it,
By *Homer*, or *Hefiod*, or—fome ancient Poet,
That th' Immortals do Names peculiarly chufe
For Perfons, and Things, which poor Mortals mayn't
    ufe.
In Submiffion to this (the Poets *Credenda,*)
I call her *Maria,* whom the God calls *Amanda.*
His Language much differs from mine, as I find,
I can't equal him, tho' I've ne'er fo much Mind.
But, 'caufe I can't fing to *Apollo*'s own Lute,
—What Woman can bear it ! I'm decree'd to be
    mute.

    And muft my Lyre for e'er remain unftrung?
    And muft *Maria* never grace my Song ?
Suppofe fhe commands me, as lately fhe did,
Muft I difobey her ?—Ye Mufes forbid !

                        What!

But if they'll not affift me, I know what muft
    follow;

I'll write,—as I have done—in Spite of *Apollo.*

❀❀❀❀❀❀❀❀❀❀❀❀ ❀❀❀❀❀❀❀❀❀❀ ❀❀❀❀

On Mr NASH's *Picture at full Length,
between the Bufts of Sir* ISAAC NEW-
TON, *and Mr* POPE.

I.

THE old *Ægyptians* hid their Wit
    In Hieroglyphick Drefs,
To give Men Pains to fearch for it,
  And pleafe themfelves with Guefs.

II.

Moderns to tread the felf fame Path,
  And exercife our Parts,
Place Figures in a Room at *Bath* ·
  Forgive them, God of Arts ·

R   III. *Newton*

III.

Newton, if I can judge aright,
　All Wifdom doth exprefs;
His Knowledge gives Mankind new Light,
　Adds to their Happinefs.

IV.

Pope is the Emblem of true Wit,
　The Sun-fhine of the Mind;
Read o'er his Works for Proof of it,
　You'll endlefs Pleafure find.

V.

Naf? reprefents Man in the Mafs,
　Made up of Wrong and Right;
Sometimes a Knave, fometimes an Afs,
　Now blunt, and now polite.

VI.

The Picture, plac'd the Bufts between,
　Adds to the Thought much Strength,
Wifdom, and Wit are little feen,
　But Folly's at full Length.

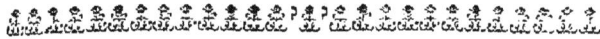

To Mifs W-------MS, *Maid of Honour to
the late* Queen.

HAIL, lovely Maid, whom Heav'ns ordain
  To fhine in *Caiolina's* Train !
When you her high Commands obey,
The Graces their Attendance pay;
When you the duteous Task perfue,
Obfequious they appeai in you
For each engaging Grace is feen,
Confpicuous in your Form and Mien.

  Defcendant of a gloiious Race,
Who oft the *Britifh* Crown did grace .
Ere here the conqu'ring Eagles flew,
Ere Roman Arms or Arts we knew ,
Long they maintain'd their Country fiee,
Nor yielded but to Fate's Decree.

R 2   Subdu'd

Subdu'd at laſt the Homage paid,

And *Saxon* Kings and Laws obey'd ,

'Twas then a Bard from *Merlin* ſprung,

Thus to his Harp prophetick ſung.

" From *Cambrian* Race a Nymph ſhall riſe,

" Bright as yon *Venus* of the Skies ;

" Whence *Romulus* or *Brutus* came,

" Who gave to *Rome* and *Britain* Name

" As *Pallas* wiſe, as *Cynthia* chaſte,

" With ſparkling Bloom like *Hebe* grac'd ,

" She in the *Britiſh* Court ſhall ſhine,

" In Beauty next the *Brunſwick* Line,

" To that Great Queen Attendance pay,

" Whoſe Birth ſhall honour * *David*'s Day.

" This Nymph our Glory ſhall retrieve,

" Receive that Homage which we give,

" They us ſubdued by Arms and Arts ;

" She ll make Repriſals on their Hearts.

" Let

* The firſt of March, St *David*, the Patron of *Wales*

" Let Bards prepare fublimeft Lays,

" And to their Harps refound her Praife,

" To lateft Times tranfmit her Fame,

" And *A———a W—ll—ms* be her Name.

ON

*Reading fome Differtations, in the
Reverend Dr* FOULKES's *modern An-
tiquities.*

SOME will, perhaps, think they've a Right to
  blame,

When to thefe Lines they fee a Woman's Name.

Why fhou'd I then obnoxious Praife beftow,

And unavailing Honour ftrive to fhew ?

Well then, —left I fhou'd prejudice the Caufe,

And draw a Cenfure, by my weak Applaufe;

I'll not attempt the panegyrick Strain,

Nor fond expatiate on this Work, in vain ·

Be

Be that the Province of judicious Friends :
To fay—I'm pleas'd—is all my Mufe pretends.

A *Cambro-Britton* muft with Pleafure trace
The Means which Heav'n ordain'd to fave our Race,
Tho', in the Fight, our warlike Fathers prov'd
Fierce as their Wolves, and as our Rocks unmov'd,
Yet Heav'n be prais'd that here, the Eagles flew,
And *Roman* Arts that Fiercenefs cou'd fubdue,
That Laws prevail'd, which their juft Rights main-
   tain'd ,
And but from favage Liberty reftrain'd !

Still honour'd by our Sex, ftill dear to Fame,
Be the firft *Edwards* great, and glorious Name!
Who abrogated that unrighteous Power,
By which our Sex enjoy'd nor Land nor Dower.
No Wonder for this Prince the much-lov'd Wife
Should rifque her own to fave his dearer Life!

(The

(The Surgeon's Art, when ineffectual found,)
Shou'd brave e'en Death, and suck the poison'd
‘ Wound!

Let Fame to latest Times his Virtues tell,
And own his Laws, our *Howel Dda*'s excel!

Superior Blessings, still, to us allow'd,
See! pure Religion breaking thro' a Cloud,
The Mist of SUPERSTITION clear'd away,
Diffusive shine in her own Heav'nly Ray!

May Rage, and Ignorance, attempt in vain
To rule our Temples, or our Courts again ;
And may their horrid Offspring, here no more,
Glut *her* fierce Thirst, with Draughts of human
    Gore.
May *Britons* ne'er the hellish Fury feel,
Her Chains, her Whips, her Gibbets, Fire, or Wheel!

But

But blefs'd with equal Laws, and Gofpel Light,
May Peace, and Charity, their Hearts unite !

O Heav'n-defcended Charity ! 'tis thine
To rule our Spirits, and our Hearts refine.
Th' angelick Miffion Thou ! can'ft beft inftill ;
" To God give Glory, and to Men Goodwill "
Thy divine Spirit if we can't attain,
Our Hope's ill-grounded, and our Faith is vain.
The grand *Criterion*, Thou ! celeftial Grace !
Of the Difciples of the Prince of Peace.
For Thee ! a new Commandment we receive !
(He, both the Precept, and th' Example gave ,)
" Love one another," The bleft Saviour faid.
O *Britons* ! let the Mandate be obey'd.

VERSES

VERSES *to her* Daughter.

With Dr CARTER's *Sermons.*

O Thou ' whofe Welfare as my own I prize,
    Regard the Inftruction of the Learn'd and
      Wife.
Such muft this Author be, who writes fo well;
Whofe Method, Doctrine, Senfe, and Style excel.
As thefe Difcourfes the beft Rules impart,
May'ft thou, my Dear ' infcribe them on thy Heart '
Reduce to Practice ev'ry Precept here,
And in the Paths of Virtue perfevere !

  No fiery Flafhes, here, of zealous Rage,
No Fumes of Bigotry obfcure the Page,
No wild enthufiaft Flights pervert the Text;
Nor is the Senfe by fceptic Doubts perplext

S

But

But Reafon's Pow'r is feen in cleareft Light,
And Gofpel Truth appears divinely bright.

The Merit of thofe Sermons ftands confeft ;
Whofe Arguments can bear a Reader's Teft.
No Grace of Action, or Deliv'ry, there,
Engage the Paffions, or enchant the Ear.
The Preacher, ftript of all exterior Aid,
By Reafon's Force alone can then perfuade.

Our learned Author, by *that Force*, fucceeds ,
Nor Elocution, he, nor Action needs.
But potent Truth, without the Roftrum Art,
Informs the Judgment, and improves the Heart.

His Arguments are in a clofe-linkt Chain,
Strong, clear, conclufive, elegant and plain.
The moral Character he well defines ,
Thro' ev'ry Page the Chriftian Spirit fhines.

This to the Merit of the Work is due;

The Preacher quite unknown to me and you.

I, with Delight, have read, 'tis now my Care,

That you fo rational a Pleafure fhare.

You'll find an Entertainment thro' the Whole,

Where Wifdom's facred Dictates feaft the Soul.

J B.

CONTENT. *A* S O N G

Tune, *Gently touch the Warbling Lyre.*

I.

LOVELY, lafting Peace of Mind
Gently footh my Soul to Reft;
In thy foft Balm Relief we find
To heal the forrow-wounded Breaft;
'Tis Thou can'ft tune my Soul to Peace,
And make each jarring Paffion ceafe.

II. Sweet

II

Sweet Content' thou dear Delight,

   Thou sov'reign Cordial for our Woes,

Thou mak'ft our Cares and Burthens light,

   From thee inceffant Sweetnefs flows.

From Envy, Pride, and Difcord free,

We here enjoy a Heaven in Thee

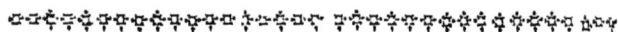

The DREAM.

In Imitation of fome Parts of Chaucer's *Second
and Third Book of Fame.*

The Introduction.

CRITICKS be kind ' this Piece forbear,

   There's nothing worth your Malice here;

'Twon't bear your Teft, I pray, don't try it,

But let a Woman dream in Quiet.

A Poet

A Poet here might fhew his Skill,
And half a dozen Pages fill,
With fine Defcription of the Scene,
Where he had been a Napping ta'en.
His Reader he awake might keep,
By telling, when he fell afleep ;
Which, doubtlefs, muft be in the Spring,
When Nightingales, and Linnets fing,
And he, on flow'ry Bank, was laid,
Where Bays, and Myrtle mix their Shade ;
Where Odours wafted from each Breeze,
And *Zephirs* whifper'd thro' the Trees ·
Where the cool, limpid, purling Stream,
With Murmurs foft, prolong'd the Dream.

All this, and more, full well I know it,
Might be perform'd by a Male Poet,
Defcriptions I muft lay afide,
I flept, and dreamt at the Fire-fide :

Tho'

Tho' Men in Fields may sleep or roam,
Women had best to nap at Home.

But ere I tell my strange Adventure,
Or Regions visionary enter ,
'Tis fit, I, like poetick Folk,
Shou'd *Phœbus*, or some Muse invoke.
I'll do't for Form, tho' Truth to tell,
A Dish of Tea inspires as well.

Ye Maids, who on *Parnassus* sing,
And haunt the *Heliconian* Spring '
Aid me to tell my Dream aright,
And animate me in my Flight!

O *Phœbus* ' help, I thee implore,
I ne'er was on the Wing before;
Assist to bring each Track to view,
Thro' which thy Father's Eagle flew

The DREAM.

I Took up *Chaucer* t'other Day,
  To pafs fome irkfome Hours away;
When I his Book of Fame had read,
(Which fure with Whimfeys fill'd my Head,)
Morpheus, the Sleep-compelling God,
Soon charm'd me with his leaden Rod.
My Reafon bound in Sleep's foft Chain,
Ungovein'd Fancy ftrait grew vain,
Bore me, where Antiquaries found
A *Roman* Fort, on *Britifh* Ground.
Methought, I breath'd the Ev'ning Air,
Upon the Summit of * *Mole-gare* ,
Much pleas'd I was, and gazing ftood,
While the *Welfh* Hills, and *Irifh* Flood,

With

* *Mole gare,* a Hill in the County of *Flint*

With various Profpects, greet my Eyes,
And well-known Scenes, promifcuous rife.

From thence * *Mole-Arthur* I behold,
Where the fam'd *Britton* fat of Old,
His Four-and-twenty Knights among ,
(As *Cimbrian* Bards have whilome fung)
If any at this Tale will mock,
Let them repair to view the Rock,
Where, if to count twice Twelve they're able,
They'll find the Seats of the Round Table.

' *Halkin ton* Hills, the *Welch Peru*,
Big with their Ore, rife next to view

Lo ! where fair *Winifreda* fell,
Whofe Blood produc'd a Holy Well
Hail ! Virgin Saint, may nought that's vile
Thy facred Fountain e'er defile'

S:

---

* *Mole-Arthur*, a Hill in *Derbyshire*

See *Flint* ¹ unhappy *Richard* there
Was made a Prey to *Lancaster*.

O'er *Offa's* Dyke, I haste my Sight,
To view my former dear Delight;
There *Alyn* glides, thro' flow'ry Meads,
There fertile Fields, and pleasing Shades:
Yonder the much-lov'd Spot of Earth
That gave forlorn *Melissa* Birth!
New crouding Thoughts my Brain oppreſt,
And Paſſions ſtruggl'd in my Breaſt.
Such Vi'lence would have broke Sleep's Chain,
If Fancy had not chang'd the Scene.
Quick, ſhe preſents old *Jeffrey's* Fable,
His wild Conceits, and ſpeaking Eagle;
And a romantick Scene prepar'd
To mimick that in the old Bard.

T   Ar

An Eagle of prodigious Size,

Methought, defcended from the Skies,

His foarding Pinions wing thro' Air,

And down he lights on dear *Mok-gore*

His Feathers fhone like buinifh'd Gold,

With Wonder I his Form behold

When, in the Twinkling of an Eye,

He fiz'd me, and away did fly

Some here, perhaps, their Jeft won't lofe,

But fay me, like *Reynard*'s Goofe,

Or, afk me, if I rode aftride?

No, I moft decently did ride,

And upright fat on th' Eagle's Back,

When thus, to my Surprize, he fpake,

" Pr'ythee, take Heart, b' affur'd of this,

Nought fhall betide Thee that's amifs

And now, I may declare my Name,

Where thou firft go, and whence I came,

Attend

Attend my Speech—*Jove*'s Eagle, I,

Commanded hence with Thee to fly.

Too much thou haft thyfelf confin'd,

Thou feldom doft relax thy Mind

Thy Book, and Needle can't delight,

From eight at Morn, 'till nine at Night.

T' amufe Thee now my Care muft be,

(So *Jove*'s immutable Decree')

I'll bear Thee to the Houfe of Fame,

(Sufpend thy female Fears for Shame')

The Temple's in the middle Way,

Exactly 'twixt Heaven, Earth, and Sea

There I, with Thee, muft wing my Flight,

While Wonders open to thy Sight"

With that, his Flight he upwards took,

And downwards bade me caft a Look,

Then down I look'd on Hills, and Dales,

On flow'ry Fields, and fmiling Vales,

On glitt'ring Spires, and verdant Woods,

On floating Ships, and rolling Floods.

But foon thefe vanifh'd from my Eyes,

So fwift he brufh'd thro' yielding Skies.

Our Earth no bigger than a Bead

Seem'd to my Eye; when thus he faid,

" Difmifs thy Fears, turn up thy Face,

Behold this wide extended Space.

The Sun will foon withdraw his Light,

And leave the Moon to rule the Night.

The glitt'ring Stars will then appear,

And fpangle o'er the Hemifpheie,

Lo ! *Vefper* leads the radiant Train

T' adorn, like Gems, th' ætherial Plain.

No Telefcope thou'lt need to fee

What brightens o'er the *Galaxy*.

Behold ! the circling *Milky-Way*

Its ftarry Pavement there difplay,

Auriga's ftormy Kids fee there,

And *Caffiopeia* in her Chair,

Great

Great *Perseus* with *Medusa's* Head,

And *Cygnus* here his Wings doth spread;

The *Argo* there in *Æther* sails,

His hideous Form there *Scorpio* trails;

Yonder, ambitious *Phaeton* drove ;

(Unhappy Proof of *Phœbus'* Love ')

The Youth, by *Scorpio* terrify'd,

No more the fiery Steeds could guide,

Jove, at his Head, the Light'ning hurl'd,

And struck him dead, to save the World.

Lo ' here an Instance that a Fool

Should not be suffer'd to bear Rule."

Then upwards still he wing'd his Way,

While I the wide Expanse survey

Then I reflected in my Mind

On what we in *Boetius* find,

How that a vig'rous Thought may fly

On Feathers of *Philofophy* ,

May

May thro' celeſtial Regions ſoar,
And all the ſtarry *Orbs* explore

Th' Imperial Bird his Pinions ply'd ,
At laſt, ſtupendous loud, he cry'd,
" Thy Heart reſume , now all is well ,
Look up and ſee, here's *Bonne Hoſtell* !
Write what thou ſee'ſt, and ſo, *Adieu*,"
And then away from me he flew.

On a high Rock appear'd the Pile,
Th' Aſcent not gain'd without much Toil .
The Rock was bright, and ſmooth as Glaſs,
I wonder'd of what Stone it was ,
And found at laſt, to my Surprize,
'Twas not of Adamant, but Ice.
Here on the Rock engrav'd I ſaw
Some Names preſerv d from Storms, and Thaw.
But the moſt part were quite eraz'd
By Heat, or hoſtile Time defac'd.

Tho' fome as clear, and perfect were,

As if but newly graven there ,

Nor Heat, nor Storms could thefe invade,

Protected by the Temple's Shade

Thefe Names thro' num'rous Ages paft,

And with the Dome itfelf, fhall laft.

    On this Foundation I beheld

The tow'ring Structure, which excell'd

The boafted Works of *Greece* or *Rome*,

Or the more fam'd *Ephefian* Dome

The Walls were all of *Beryl* Stone,

Which with amazing Luftre fhone.

Four brazen Gates I there defcry,

Facing each Quarter of the Sky

I enter, and, amaz'd, behold

The *Jafper* Floor, and Roof of Gold.

Th' impending Lamps inceffant glow,

And ever-living Light beftow.

There Heroes of a fabl'd Race
The Weftern Wall, in Statues, grace;
Alcides, in his fhaggy Spoil,
Seems there to reft from all his Toil.
And there great *Perfeus* was beheld,
Tremendous, with *Minerva*'s Shield.
Here *Linus*, there *Mufæus* ftands,
And each his filver Harp commands.
There *Orpheus* plays, and Trees around
Dancing obey the magick Sound.
His living Lyre *Amphion* tries,
And ftrait the *Theban* Walls arife.

On the North-fide, with Trophies crown'd,
Were *Gothick* Heroes, once renown'd.
Great *Woden* there his Spear doth wield,
And *Runick* Figures grac'd his Shield.
Scythian Philofophers appear,
Abaris, *Anacharfis* there,

Zamolxis

Zamolxis high above the Reft ·
Thefe *Bards* and *Druids* were expreft.

The Eaftern Wall, with Gems, and Gold,
And Di'monds glorious to behold,
Shew'd *Belus*, *Ninus*, and the Train,
Who the Term *Magi* did obtain.
Confucius there, the learn'd and good ,
And there the wife *Chaldeans* ftood
Thefe Sages fix'd the Solar Year,
And could defcribe each radiant Sphere.
Here *Zoroafter* waves his Wand
And *Brachmans* there the Moon command.

Of *Egypt*'s Priefts, on the South-fide,
A venerable Train I fpy'd.
Great *Trefmigiftus* then appear'd,
For fublime Truths, and Arts rever'd.
Here proud *Sefoftris* ftrikes with Awe,
Whom fcepter'd Slaves are forc'd to draw.

U   There

There *Amafis*, in Triumph plac'd;
The whole with Hieroglyphicks grac'd

See! Pillars in bright Order fhow,
The Capitals with Jewels glow.
Here *Cyrus*, there the Hero ftood
Who dar'd th' impetuous *Granick* Flood
Leonidas, the brave and bold,
And fweet-foul'd *Cimon*, I behold.
Th' Imperial Hero, on a Throne
Adorn'd with Trophies, greatly fhone.
Near to th' immortal *Cæfar* ftood
That *Brutus*! too feverely good!
Unconquer'd *Cato* there was plac'd,
And the young Victor, brave and chafte,
Scipio, who only could fubdue
The * Warrior, who next ftrikes my View.

Nor

* *Hannibal*

Nor fighting Chiefs alone were there,
But learned Sages too appear
Lycurgus, *Solon* there I find,
Whose equal Laws reclaim'd Mankind.
The *Samian*, and the *Stagyrite*,
With *Socrates* for ever bright.
And there, as oft in *Rome* before,
The *Civick* Crown great *Tully* wore.
Immortal *Plato* too was seen,
With Brow sedate, and easy Mien
Great *Aristarchus* pleas'd I view'd,
Whose System Moderns have renew'd.
The *Syracusian* * Artist there
Held in his Hand his wond'rous Sphere.

Around the Centre then appear'd,
Above the Rest, eight Columns rear'd

High

* *Archimedes*

High on the first, enthron'd in Gold,
Sat mighty *Homer* blind, and bold
His Head with facred Fillets bound,
Troy's Wars adorn'd the Pillar round.
There fighting Deities engage,
There *Trojans* fly *Achilles'* Rage;
From *Hector* there the *Greeks* retreat,
Here *Troy* in *Hector* yields to Fate

Majeftick in a Silver Sarine,
Where well-fet Gems refplendent fhine,
Great *Maro* fat, around his Head
Laurc's in golden Foliage fpread
In Sculpture on the Pillars feen
The pious Chief, the dying Queen,
The *Latian* Wars, the *Elyzian* Plain,
And Heroes doom'd in *Rome* to reign

Next hanging on the bafe ftruck my Sight,
His Seat of Steel was polifh'd bright,

Tranfported

Tranfported between Wrath and Heat,

He feem'd to totter on his Seat.

There might I on the Column trace

The unhappy End of *Cadmus'* Race.

Infpir'd with mad, and direful Rage,

Th' impious Brothers there engage,

There little *Tydeus*, great with Ire,

Makes Forty nine to *Styx* retire.

Gigantick *Dryas*, with fierce Joy,

There kills the fair *Arcadian* Boy.

   High on a Throne of fhining Brafs,

Afpiring *Lucan* feated was ;

His ftately Port, exalted Air

Impetuous Youth, and Fire declare.

Here, with bold Strokes, the Artift grav'd

Pharfalia's Field, and *Rome* enflav'd.

There haplefs *Pompey*, vanquifh'd flies ,

On *Egypt's* Shore, there, headlefs lies.

                       Great

Great *Cæfar* leap'd into the Waves,

There all the *Pharian* Fury braves ·

One Hand his faithful Annals held,

And one his Sword, which plow'd the liquid Field.

Of *Claudian* then a View I took,

Serene his Air, sublime his Lock ,

The Column with nice Sculpture grac'd

Here *Proferpine*, by *Pluto* plac'd,

Affrighted in the Chariot rode,

Tho' footh'd by the relentless God

There *Venus*, in her *Cyprian* Court,

And little Loves, and Graces fport.

Then witty *Ovid* next is feen,

With graceful Eafe, and courtly Mien

The World's firft Rife, and Bodies chang'd

Aound the polifh'd Pillar rang'd.

Behold

Behold *Anacreon*! tuneful Bard!
Much fafer to be feen than heard
While Mirth fits fparkling in his Eyes,
His foft bewitching Lyre he tries
Gay *Bacchus* danc'd with Ivy crown'd,
And fmiling Loves the Bard furround.

There *Pindar* ftrikes his founding Lyre,
The Figure fpeaks his Force and Fire,
There the prefiding * Deities
Survey the Games from Azure Skies
The Games of *Greece* the Column grace,
There the fwift rapid Chariot Race,
The Champions caft the Bar and Spear,
And winged Feet contending there,
The Steed appears each Nerve to ftrain,
To bear his Mafter o'er the Plain.

The

* *Jupiter, Neptune, Apollo* and *Hercules*

The Victors in each Exercife,

Met at the Goal, receive the Prize

Thefe Pillars, in a Circle plac'd,

Surround a Throne where Jewels blaz'd,

Whofe mingl'd Rays, and various Light

At once confound and pleafe the Sight.

Di'monds their ing Luftre fhow,

And flaming Rubies feem to glow,

There Amed ts their purple Rays,

And Saphirs their bright Azure blaze

The Topaz cafts a golden Dye,

And Em'ralds there revive the Eye

Here proud Imperial Fame, in State,

To hear her Vot'ies was fate

When firft on her I caft my Eyes,

She feem'd but of a dwarfifh Size,

No fooner had I fix'd my View,

To a gigantick Form fhe grew

With her the Dome, and Columns rife,
And tow'ring feem t' invade the Skies.
A thoufand Plumes the Goddefs bears,
A thoufand curious lift'ning Ears,
A thoufand wakeful prying Eyes,
A thoufand Tongues, inceffant, fhe employs.

Around her high Imperial Seat,
The Mufes all in Order wait ;
For her they fing, and tune the Lyre,
And noble Thoughts, and Verfe infpire.

While I thefe Wonders view'd around,
Methought, I heard the Trumpet found ;
When ftrait, thick as the fwarming Bees,
That fally out in Colonies,
Promifcuous Throngs the Temple croud,
And make their Claim to Fame aloud.
From every Region there they came,
To pay their Homage to the Dame.

X

The

The Young, the Old, the Rich, the Poor,

In fuppliant Crowds her Grace implore.

Some fhe rejected with a Frown,

And fome fhe did with Honours crown.

Merit fhe oft would difregard,

And oft the Worthlefs wou'd reward:

So, her blind Sifter Fortune rules,

Gives Rags to th' Wife, and Robes to Fools.

   The Sons of Learning there attend ,

Who to her Favours firft pretend .

Madam, your Juftice we implore,

Confirm our Fame, we ask no more:

Rewarded only with Renown,

Let deathlefs Fame our Labours crown.

She fmil'd , 'tis fit your Names fhould live,

Who deathlefs Fame to others give ;

Who Nature's Myfteries explore,

And thro' each ftarry Region foar.

The golden Trump, ye Mufes, raife !

Proclaim in tuneful Notes their Praife.

Thro' the wide World the Notes were heard;

And All th' harmonious Sound rever'd.

Then Odours all their Sweets diffufe ;

Nor op'ning Flow'rs, nor rofy Dews,

Nor Gales from *Africk*'s Spicy Coaft,

Could e'er fuch balmy Fragrance boaft.

While the learn'd Train attentive ftood,

The Dame, with fweet Complacence, view'd

Two more confpicuous than the Reft ;

And gently bowing, thus addreft :

" *Milton*, and *Newton*, my beft lov'd !

" Juftly 'bove all my Sons approv'd ;

" When firft I rais'd this Dome of State,

" I vow'd ; and *Jove* confirm'd its Fate:

" None in this Dome enthron'd appears,

" Without my Teft, a thoufand Years !

When

" When twice five Cent'ries are expir'd,

" And You thro' each learn'd Age admir'd ;

" Seats, next my own, shall be prepar'd

" For Thee, great Sage ! and Thee, O sacred Bard !"

Then a small Tribe the Dame addrest,

And thus preferr'd their strange Request ;

' Great Goddess ! by Mankind ador'd,

' To us our humble Wish afford.

' We're not solicitous for Fame,

' Conceal our Labours and our Name.

' Virtue alone we did regard;

' Let Virtue be our sole Reward.'

" These Folk are mad ' (enrag'd she cries,)

" Dare you immortal Fame despise ?

" I'll to the wond'ring World reveal

" Those Virtues which you would conceal ;

" The golden Trumpet, with Renown,

" Shall all your pious Actions crown :

Strong

Strong were the Notes, yet fweet and clear,
And grateful Scents perfum'd the Air.

To thefe another Band fucceed;
Who, confcious of their Merit, plead;
'Since living Virtue is defpis'd,
'Now let our Works be juftly priz'd:
We for good Fame have done our part,
'Vouchfafe to crown our juft Defert.'
Frowning; fhe thus rejects their Claim,
" Scandal, and ignominious Fame
" Be Yours "—The Trump of Slander founds,
And with harfh Notes their Honour wounds.
From the black rufty Clarion broke
Offenfive Scents, and Clouds of Smoke,
Encreafing ftill where'er they went,
To blaft the haplefs Innocent.

But

But now a more fuccefsful Train

Humbly approach the facred Fane.

Thefe, like the former Troop, their Days

Had wholly fpent in Virtue's Ways.

To thefe the Dame—" It is my Will,

" That your Renown the World fhould fill;

" Tho' I rejected the juft Claim

" Of thofe who merit equal Fame;

" Virtue herfelf would lofe her Crown,

" Should fhe too boldly claim Renown.

" Unask'd, I'll now beftow on you

" A Recompence beyond your Due."

Then, thro' th' applauding World, their Praife

The fweet melodious Trump conveys.

Now an embroider'd Troop appears,

With fmart Toupees, and fparkifh Airs;

The

'The Fame to which we moft afpire;

'And of your Majefty defire,

'Is to be thought of Confequence

'Among the Fair, whofe Innocence

'We ne'er have wrong'd, unlefs in Rumour,

'To fhew our Wit, and fprightly Humour.

'We care not who their Favours claim,

'Provided we may rob their Fame.'

" I grant you your Petition, Beaus;

" Each Blaft a Lady fhall expofe."

Encourag'd at this ftrange Succefs,

A Crowd of Fops around her prefs;

'Fair Queen! we humbly beg you'd pleafe

'To favour us no lefs than thefe.'

" Coxcombs ! (fhe cry'd) avoid the Place,

" The foul-mouth'd *Clarion* fhall you grace,"

In ev'ry Note was fomething new,

That ridicul'd this foppifh Crew :

Then

Then Jefts, and Scoffs, were heard aloud,
And Laughter ran thro' all the Crowd.

A Troop of martial Worthies came,
Who fought for Liberty, not Fame.
Juft Heroes, who efpous'd the Caufe
Of dear Religion and the Laws.
" Live you (fhe faid) in my bright Roll!
" Your Fame I'll found from Pole to Pole.
" A Flourifh there '—be thefe renown'd,
" And lateft Times their Praife refound."

Then came another warlike Train,
Who glory'd in vaft Numbers flain.
' For Thee, O Goddefs! we deftroy
' Our Species, with invidious Joy;
' Relentlefs fwim thro' Streams of Blood,
' For Thee, our chief, our only Good!'
" Ye flaught'ring Fools from hence retire,
" Dare you to lafting Fame afpire?

" Your Deeds fhall in Oblivion lie,

" And all your blafted Glories die."

Of Patriots now an awful Cro wd

Before the Goddefs humbly bow'd

With thefe a Crew did flily mix,

Skill'd in dark Plots and Politicks.

They in a lucky Moment came ;

The giddy undifcerning Dame

Rewards alike their diff 'rent Pleas,

And bids the Trumpet found their Praife.

While thefe employ'd my Ears and Eyes,

Methought, I heard a fudden Noife,

Like diftant Floods, when Tempefts roar,

And Billows beat the hollow Shore .

Or Sounds, which from afar are fent,

Of rolling Thunder, almoft fpent.

Strait by fome Pow'r I was convey'd,

Where I another Dome furvey'd .

Y

With

With rapid Force it whirl'd around;

And thence proceeded all the Sound·

Nor Silence here, nor Reft, nor Peace,

The Noife and Hurry never ceafe.

As many Doors, and Windows here,

As Leaves on Trees in *May* appear·

Thefe Day and Night are open found,

Still pervious to receive the Sound;

As Needles tremble t'wards the Pole,

As to the Sea the Rivers roll;

As Flame and Smoke will upwards fly,

And mounting feek the diftant Sky,

As weighty Bodies downwards tend,

So hither muft all Sound afcend.

A Stone, when caft into a Lake,

Will ftrait a trembling Circle make;

The Water, by that Motion ftir'd,

Will fpread a Second, then a Third;

Still

Still round each Ring another's made,
Till each the Margin does invade.

Thus Voice, or Sound, impels the Air,
And makes an ambient Ringlet there,
Which undulating will enforce
Another Circle in its Courſe,
Each Ring will ſtill another drive,
At *Rumour's Houſe* till all arrive

Of various News I much did hear,
Of Sickneſs, Health, of Peace and War;
Of Love and Hate, of Death and Life,
Of Reconcilements, and of Strife;
Of rich exhauſtleſs Minerals,
Of Shipwrecks, and of ſtranded Whales,
Of flaming Meteors which appear,
Like Armies fighting in the Air;
Of Towns, by Fire in Aſhes loſt,
Of Navies on the Ocean toſt,

Of

Of Famine, Plenty, Lofs and Gain,

Of Thunder, Hurricanes and Rain ;

Of *India* Stock, and *South Sea* Schemes,

Of Apparitions, and ftrange Dreams ;

Of *Lilliputian* Potentate,

Of Broils, and Factions in the State ;

Of Miracles vouch'd by the Pope,

Of Wives who from their Mates elope,

Of jilted Swains, of Nymphs beguil'd,

Of monftrous Births, and Men with Child :

Of thefe they talk'd, with ceafelefs Noife,

And fometimes mingl'd Truth with Lies.

Above, below, within, without,

Appear'd a moft diforder'd Rout.

There Troops of Travellers I faw,

Quacks and Practitioners in Law;

Of Party Zealots a large Crew,

Of Politicians not a few,

A Band

A Band of Sage Aftrologers,
Converfant with the Signs and Stars;
In num'rous Throngs Projectors preft
The grand Elixir full in Queft.

Some whifper'd Secrets in the Ear,
Some fpoke aloud, that all might hear;
When one did fome new Tale relate,
Another foon would more repeat .
The Rumour gather'd, as it flew,
On ev'ry Tongue it larger grew:
To Eaft, and Weft, and North, and South
News ftill encreas'd from Mouth to Mouth.

Thus, from a Spark, the quick'ning Fire
Will blazing to the Clouds afpire;
Th' impetuous Flames will curling fly,
Till fpacious Towns in Ruin lie.

Oft

Oft in fome narrow Paffage there,
A Truth, and Lie, contending were ,
So clofe were they together pent,
Dubious a while appear'd th' Event ,
The Struggle 'till at laft they end,
And Truth, and Lie, together blend :
Infeparably now combin'd,
They fly together in the Wind.

Aloft the Imperial Phantom fate
To point their Courfe, and fix their Date .
Some fhe appoints fhould long abide,
Some muft immediately fubfide ,
Some, like the Moon, fhe does ordain
Alternately to wax, or wane.
Millions of winged Wonders fly,
Scatter'd o'er Earth, and Seas, and Sky.

Intent

Intent I ſtood to hear, and ſee,

When one, methought, thus whiſper'd me—

' How didſt Thou to yon Place aſcend ?

' Thou wilt not, ſure ! to Fame pretend'

" No;—let me have but a good Name ;

" I will not make Pretence to Fame.

" Would Heaven, indulgent to my Pray'r,

" Relieve my Mind from anxious Care;

" A mod'rate Competency give,

" Obſcure, unknown, I'd chuſe to live.

" And if, unbent, my Thoughts ſometime

" Should gently flow in harmleſs Rhyme :

" Let *Wymondſold* approve my Lays,

" I'll court no Fame, nor wiſh for higher Praiſe

To

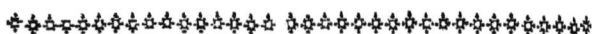

✤✦✤✦✤✦✤✦✤✦✤✦✤✦ ✤✦✤✦✤✦✤✦✤✦✤✦✤✦✤✦

To Mr Y------KE.

THE twenty ninth of *January*, you fay,
    You'll always note as a propitious Day,
Since, on that Day, fome twenty Years ago,
Your Friend had the beft Gift Heav'n could beftow;
A pleafing Theme, no doubt,—but 'twas my Fate,
On the fame Day and Year, to change my happy
      State.

Need I fay more?— or need you, Sir, be told,
Heav'n had not for each Maid a *Wymondfold* '
Tho' for the favour'd one it did provide
The dear Companion and the faithful Guide;
The Friend, the Husband, and the Lover too,
Sincere, indulgent, tender, fond, and true.
Still may his dear deferving Choice poffefs,
Still merit, her tranfcendent Happinefs.

                              Still

Still may fhe, as a Crown to him, appear,

With whofe high Price ev'n Rubies can't compare.

Of virtuous Daughters many have done well;

But fhe the moft excelling does excel.

Such is fair *Wymondfold*. — — — —

     —Such may fhe be,

Whom Heav'n indulgent has in Store for Thee!

     The

THE

ROYAL HERMITAGE:

A

P O E M.

Written in the Year 1733.

On the BUSTOES *in the* ROYAL HERMITAGE.

WHILE to our QUEEN each duteous Bard conveys

The faithful Tribute of exalted Praise,

While Genius, Learning, all their Force com-
bine

To make the Numbers, as the Theme, divine;

How shall a *Cambrian Muse*, obscure, and mean,

The lowest, latest, of the tuneful Train,

Too weak her Wings, too tardy in her Flight,

Amongst their Sterling Coin, dare to present her
Mite?

O *Queen* !

O *Queen!* more learn'd than e'er *Britannia* saw,
Since our fam'd *Tudor* to the Realm gave Law.
O *Wife!* more happy in thy Lord alone
Than in the Pow'r, and Splendor, of his Throne.
O *Mother!* bleſt in your Illuſtrious Race,
The Guardian Angels of our future Peace.
O *Patroneſs of Science!* wilt thou deign
T' accept from thy own Sex this artleſs Strain?
Around the Throne too dazling Glories dwell,
May I, moſt gracious *Queen!* approach thy Cell?

Hail happy *Grotto!* to thy bleſt Retreat
Greatneſs retires to be more truly Great.
Here, by the Sculptor's Art, are well deſign'd
The *Buſts* of Thoſe, who dignify'd their Kind.
Locke, *Boyle*, and *Newton*, *Woolaſton*, and *Clarke*,
Brighten thoſe Paths which Ignorance made dark,
Reaſon, and Arts, Truth moral, and divine,
In their immortal Works, unclouded ſhine.

Reſemblance

Refemblance the well-judging Eye delights,

And th' active Soul to femblant Thought excites :

Intent, Sh' exerts her Faculties, and Powers,

Rifes in Thought, in Contemplation towers.

Reafon, that Emanation of the Mind,

Breaks forth in *Locke* ; diffufive, and refin'd.

Wifdom, and *Piety*, their Beams unite

To fhine in *Boyle*, with ftrong, convictive Light;

Which, thro' the various Works of Nature, fhows

God, the fole Source, whence all Perfection flows.

Newton th' Allwife Creator's Works explores,

Sublimely, on the Wings of Knowledge, foars;

Th' eftablifh'd Order of each Orb unfolds,

And th' omni-prefent *God*, in all, beholds :

If to the dark Abyfs, or bright Abode

He points , the View ftill terminates in *God*

The

The moral Duties *Woolaſton* diſplays;
On Nature's Laws the firm Foundation lays.

In *Claɪke* the Chriſtian Purity appears,
Reveal'd Religion he divinely clears
From Miſts of Error, Vapours of blind Zeal,
Which oft her Heav'n-born Beauties would conceal;
From ſanguine Marks, which her pure Whiteneſs
    ſtain'd,
And all her ſacred Truths polluted, and profan'd.
Here Reaſon, Learning, primogeneal Law,
Submit to *Faith*, with Reverence and Awe.
'Tis She, *Celeſtial Grace* muſt thoſe refine;
'Tis her Impreſſion ſtamps them all divine.

  Theſe are the *Worthies*, whom our glorious
    Queen
Delights to honour in this ſolemn Scene;

Sh

She confecrates their Memory to Fame,
Affixing theirs to her own deathlefs Name.

While plenteous *Thames* flows from its Cryftal
  Urn;
While ebbing Tides to *Ocean*'s Bed return;
While circling Waves around *Britannia* move,
While Liberty, and Honour, *Britons* love;
While the fair *Moon* reflects the folar Ray,
And guides the Motions of the fwelling *Sea*;
While the bright *Sun* the golden Day fhall give,
With *Caroline*'s, thefe *Sages*' Fame will live.

A a

MERLIN.

MERLIN:

A

POEM.

Humbly infcrib'd to her MAJESTY.

The BRITONS *ever to his Lore attend,*
And but with Time itfelf his Predicts end.
The LEEK.

Written in the Year 1733.

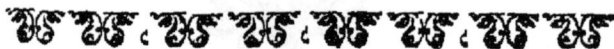

MERLIN:

A POEM.

Humbly Infcribed (*Octob.* 1735.) to

Her MAJESTY, QUEEN GUARDIAN.

ILLUSTRIOUS QUEEN!
The loyal Zeal excufe,

The fond Ambition, of a *Britifh Mufe*,

Who wou'd, in *Merlin*'s Praife, attempt to foar,

And, in his *Cave*, Your Patronage implore

Protection feek, beneath Your *Royal Name*,

And borrow Strength to rife, from *Merlin*'s Fame.

When

When *Sol* to diftant Climes had giv'n the Day,
And fhone on ours, with pale reflected Ray;
When *Night*, with folemn Pace, advanc'd her Head,
And o'er the Hemifphere her Mantle fpread,
Yet thro' the fable Gloom thofe Orbs reveal'd,
Which, in a Flood of Light, the Day conceal'd:
I, to a Summit, mus'd along to fee
Unnumber'd *Suns*, which croud the *Galaxy*.
But *Merlin's Cave* had fuch Impreffions made,
And Royal Honours to his Mem'ry pay'd;
Pleas'd with Reflection, and involv'd in Thought,
Creative *Fancy* foon this *Vifion* wrought.

Then, lo! beneath a venerable *Oak*,
Which oft repell'd the Tempeft's furious Stroke;
Whofe fpreading Arms a wide Circumf'rence fhow,
And from whofe Trunk fprings facred *Miffeltoe*.
Methought, I faw an awful *Shade* arife;
(Fit Object only for Poetick Eyes.)

The

The Form majeſtick, and the Front ſerene;

Angles, and *Circles*, on his Robe were ſeen.

The * *Northern Crown* around his Temples ſhone,

And the *Celeſtial Signs* adorn'd his Zone.

The *Britiſh Harp* ſeem'd to ſupport one Hand ;

While t'other gently wav'd the ſacred *Wand*.

The *Manes* of great *Merlin* ſtood confeſs'd ;

And my enraptur'd Fancy thus addreſs'd :

" Why will *Meliſſa* *Merlin*'s Praiſe decline,

" Diſtinguiſh'd now by Royal CAROLINE ?

" Believe not *ſuch*, as wou'd aſperſe my Name,

" But truſt thoſe *Authors*, who defend my Fame.

" You, to the Royal *Grotto*, touch'd the Lyre,

" And durſt in God-like *Newton*'s Praiſe aſpire.

" Why ſhou'd not *Britiſh Merlin* grace thy Page,

" In *Mathematicks* once eſteem'd a Sage ?

" A well-try'd *Genius* cou'd tranſmit to Fame

" My honour'd modern *Cave*, and antient *Name*

                           " Might,

* A *Conſtellation* ſo call'd

" Might, to my ROYAL GUEST, re-touch the String,

" And as * he fung the *Saint*, the *Prophet* fing.

" But fince the *Cambrian Bards* negleft the Mufe,

" *Meliffa's* humbler Strains I'll not refufe.

" Six Centuries, twice told, are now compleat,

" Since *Merlin* liv'd on this terreftial Seat.

" Knowledge appear'd, but dawning to my Sight ,

" She blaz'd on *Newton* with Meridian Light.

" Yet the faint Glimm'rings which my *Genius* taught,

" Beyond the Ken of human Art, were thought.

" What I by meer mechanick Pow'rs atchiev'd,

" Th' Effects of *Magick*, then, by moft believ'd,

" To *Stone-henge* let the Sons of Art repair,

" And view the Wonders I erected there :

" Try, if their Skill improv'd mine e'er can foil;

" Reftore the *Giants-Dance* t' *Hibernian* Soil.

" Nor in *Geometry* excell'd alone ;

" But other *Sciences* to me were known.

" I ftudy'd

* Author of the LEEK, a Poem, prefented to her Majefty

" I ftudy'd *Nature* through her various Ways;

" And chaunted to this *Harp prophetick* Lays.

" Oft to * PLINLIMON have I took my Way,

" Rofe with the *Sun*, toil'd up th' Afcent all Day;

" But fcarce could reach the Mountain's tow'ring
       Height,

" Ere radiant *Vefper* ufher'd in the Night.

" The Summit gain'd, I fought with naked Eye

" To penetrate the Wonders of the Sky.

" No Telefcopic Glafs known in that Age

" T' affift the Optics of the curious Sage.

" Tho' lov'd *Aftronomy* oft charm'd my Mind,

" I now erroneous all my Notions find.

" I thought bright *Sol* around our *Globe* had run,

" Nor knew Earth's Motion, nor the central *Sun*.

" And had I known ; could I Belief have gain'd,

" When Ignorance, and Superftition reign'd ?

B b   " Unfeen

* A Mountain in *Cardiganfhire*

" Unfeen by me, *Attraction's* mighty Force,
" And how fierce *Comets* run their ftated Courfe;
" Surprizing Scenes! by Heav'n referv'd in Store
" For its own Fav'rite *Newton* to explore.
" With Faculties enlarg'd, *He's* gone to prove
" The Laws, and Motions, of, yon *Worlds* above;
" View *Solar Syftems* in the *Milky Way,*
" And the vaft Circuits of th' Expanfe *furvey.*
" My Spirit too through Æther wings its Flight,
" Difcov'ring *Truths* deny'd my mortal Sight,
" Tranfported hovers o'er my native Ifle,
" Where Arts improve, and Peace and Plenty fmile.

" But lo! *Bootes* drives his radiant Car,
" High on its Courfe, around the *Polar Star,*
" And fiery *Draco* droops his ftarry Creft ;
" 'Tis time, thou fhouldft indulge thy needful Reft.
" Yet ftay, *Meliffa?*—try this fav'rite Lyre !
" And *Merlin* will the grateful Song infpire.

" To

" To *Learning's Patroness* my Thanks convey;

" And humbly at her Feet prefent thy Lay.

" Confcious, how mean, and how unskill'd thy Hand,

" I fee thee tremble at my kind Command.

" Let my Perfuafion, once, thy Fears beguile,

" The gracious QUEEN will condefcend to fmile

" For *Merlin*'s fake, will give *Meliffa* Leave

" To touch the Strings in my much honour'd Cave.

" And *Wallia*'s gen'rous Prince will not difdain

" What I foretell ;—tho' low, thy Lyrick Strain

To the QUEEN.

HAIL! *Guardian* of *Britannia*'s Fate,
   Whofe Worth tranfcends the Regal State '

Thee' whom propitious Heav'n defign'd

The *Guard*, and *Glory*, of thy Kind.

E'en

E'en *Juſtice* wou'd her *Pow'r Divine,*
Conſummate QUEEN ! to Thee reſign ;
Give up her *Sword* to thy Command,
And truſt her *Balance* in thy Hand,
Let happy *Britons* learn to know,
The *Queen of Virtues* reigns below!

   The Sciences, *O Royal Fair !*
Improve thro' your auſpicious Care.
Your Favour can reſtore to Fame,
From dark Oblivion, *Merlin's* Name.
The *Muſes* all to you reſort,
As to their own *Apollo's* Court.
Thrice happy *Britons !* *Wiſdom's* ſeen
Preſiding in our matchleſs QUEEN !
Aſtræa and *Minerva* join
To form one finiſh'd CAROLINE,

MERLIN'*s*

MERLIN's *Prophecy.*

Humbly inscrib'd to his Royal Highness, *the* PRINCE
of WALES.

ROYAL *FREDERICK!* *Britain's* Pride!
   Prince, for future Safety giv'n;
  For Thee 's decree'd a Virtuous *Bride,*
Choiceft *Gift* of bounteous Heav'n.

  To reward thy filial Duty,
To perpetuate *Brunfwick's* Race,
  Wit, and Learning, Youth, and Beauty,
Heav'n prepares for thy Embrace.

  No bluft'ring Storms affright the Fair,
No raging Billows dare to rife;
  Safe by *Heav'n's,* and *George's* Care,
May fhe blefs our longing Eyes!

Neptune,

Neptune, foothe old Father *Ocean* ;

Mild *Favonius,* waft thy Gales ;

 May *One* repell each threat'ning Motion,

For *Albion* t' *Other* fwell the Sails !

 Behold ! fhe comes, enrich'd with Charms,

Indulgent to thy plighted Love !

 Receive the Blefling to thy Arms,

And *Hymen's* hallow'd Rites approve.

 Illuftrious Pair ! wou'd You in Story,

Thro' fucceeding Ages, fhine ?

 Wou'd you tread the Paths to Glory ?

Follow *George,* and *Caroline* !

 And lo ! I fee a *glorious Race,*

Succeflive rifing to Renown !

 Decree'd *Britannia's* Throne to grace ;

And give new Luftre to a Crown.

        Ordain'd,

Ordain'd to wield the Sceptre Royal,

With righteous Pow'r, and gentle Sway;

    And rule o'er *Britons*, Brave, and Loyal,

'Till Heav'n, and Earth, ſhall melt away.

Mrs

Mrs WILLS *having sent a Carpet of her own Work to Mrs* MYDDEITON, *and desir'd the Ladies of* Croes-newydd, *and me, to direct our Letters for her, to be left at the Post-Office in* Okeham; *being uncertain where she shou'd be, gave Occasion to the following.*

To *Mrs* WILLS *in* England.

AS *Grecian* Wives (so *Ovid*'s Muse relates)
   Wrote long Epistles to their wand'ring Mates,
Uncertain if those Lines they e'er shou'd view;
Unknowing where they were; so I to you.

If *Rutland*'s narrow Bounds confine my Friend,
Or where the larger Liberties extend
Of ancient *Lincoln* ; whether you frequent
The Seat, where fair *Eliza*'s Youth was spent,

Beneath

Beneath wife *Harrington*'s inftructive Care ;

(Whofe Worth the weeping Marbles ftill declare)

Thee, * *Exton*, thee ! the Royal Maid did grace,

Th' illuftrious Mother of the *Brunfwick* Race.

Or are you now, † where dire inteftine Rage

Provok'd a King and People to engage ?

‖ Where *York* and *Lancafter* their Titles try'd ?

Or where the *Stowre* does *Leicefterfhire* divide ?

Wheree'er you are, to this I will impart

The faithful Dictates of a grateful Heart ;

The tender Wifh, th' Affections warm and true,

Which from one Friend are to another due.

May'ft thou, exempt from Pain, or Care, or Strife,

Infenfibly defcend the Hill of Life ;

With Thoughts unruffled, and a Mind content,

Enjoy the Comfort of a Life well-fpent.

C c   When

---

* The *Harringtons* were then poffefs'd of *Exton* now Ld *Gautfborcugh*

† *Edge hill* in *Warwickfhire*, where the firft Battle was fought between King *Charles* and his People

‖ At *Bofworth* in *Leicefterfhire*, was the laft Battle between *York* and *Lancafter*.

Where'er you dwell, howe'er employ'd you are,
If to the much-lov'd Garden you repair,
And with delight obferve the blooming Flow'rs,
Or 'twixt your Book and Work divide the Hours;
Whate'er Amufement now you may perfue,
With Pleafure here your Handy-work we view;
Where on the Carpet you with Skill difplay'd
A flow'ry Bordure, round the matchlefs Maid.
There well form'd Shades, here diff'rent Colours meet,
In various Fancies, fpread beneath her Feet.

Of the rich *Perfian* Carpets we are told,
Of Velvets, Tiffues, and their Cloths of Gold,
But fhou'd the Monarch of the glorious Eaft,
Bright as his Neighbour Sun in Splendor dreft,
Around himfelf his *India*'s Wealth difplay,
In all his orient Gems profufely gay;
And fo adorn'd fhou'd on his Carpet fhine,
His Worth cou'd ne'er amount to Her's, who fits on
    Thine!

But

But as some Knight that in the Lists of Fame,
By brave Exploits has gain'd a deathless Name;
Content with his Renown, in his great Hall,
Hangs up his Arms in Figure on the Wall.
So Thou (and sure my Fancy's not amiss !)
Shoud'st ne'er attempt another Piece like This;
But send thy Needle, Thimble, Scissars home,
To make a Figure in thy *Exton-Dome.*

ANSWER, *by Mrs* WILLS.

SO very great the Implements appear,
 You might mistake the Needle for a Spear ;
The brazen Thimble fix'd against the Wall,
On sudden View, you might a Helmet call ;
The Scissars, so magnificently great,
Seem those which of our Lives do cut the Date.

Sure

Sure thefe are Relicks ! then it might be faid,
For of fuch Trophies we have never read;
Know, thefe were us'd, where *Mira's* pleas'd to tread.

⚜⚜⚜⚜⚜⚜⚜⚜⚜⚜⚜⚜⚜⚜⚜⚜⚜⚜⚜⚜⚜⚜⚜⚜

REPLY *to Mrs* WILLS.

UNSKILFULL Conjurers, the Learned fay,
 Sometimes raife Spirits, which they cannot
  lay ;
And I, who neither Spright, nor Man can charm,
Have rais'd a Figure which may do much Harm.

How fierce th' expanded Weapon does appear !
And in the gaping Forfex ftrikes the Spear :
That one-ey'd Cyclop who the Ground has fpread,
Tremendous, fanguine Sight ! with bloody Red.
O'er its grim Head, the brazen Helmet glares,
Which tho' it neither Plumes, nor Horfetail, wears,
Yet fundry Marks of warlike Deeds it bears.

A Form

A Form fo horrid who can fhew in Verfe ?
The Hydra at the Tower looks not more fierce !

When the young *Trojan* his great Sire beheld,
In dreadful Armour ready for the Field;
Poor tim'rous *Sty*, unus'd to fuch a Sight,
Trembl'd and fhriek'd with Horror and Affright.
And who can tell what Mifchief may enfue
From the rafh Hint thoughtlefs I fent to you?
What if fome Neighbour's Child, or pregnant Wife,
Are frighten'd into Fits,—or out of Life ?
How can I anfwer for fuch dire Difafters !
Ah ' my good Friend, take care of little Mafters;
And let not little Miffes loofe their Lives,
Or tender Husbands weep for Babes, or Wives ;
But to preferve their Senfes, Lives, and Vigour,
—I beg you'll draw a Curtain o'er the Figure.

✿✿✿✿✿✿✿✿✿✿✿✿✿✿✿✿✿✿✿✿✿✿✿✿✿✿✿✿✿

To Mrs M----------N.

MADAM,

          Commiſſion'd by you, I the Liberty took

To dun a ſmart Gentleman, for your *French* Book;

Confus'd, he affirm'd, (I won't ſay he ſwore,)

'T had been in his Pocket, theſe three Months, or

      more;

Deſigning, with humble Submiſſion, to leave it,

In thoſe lilly Hands, whence he firſt did receive it.

The Book he admires, but ſuſpects 't has a Charm;

And he apprehends it has done him much Harm.

Tho' conſcious, his Duty it was, in good Manners,

Your Book to return, with his Thanks, and beſt

      Honours;

Tho'

Tho' the Day was oft fix'd on, and the Speech it
  was ready,

The Bow was well-practis'd, to approach the good
  Lady :

Tho' vaſt Preparations! yet ſtill Reſolution

Was wanting to put them in due Execution.

Himſelf to excuſe, he now ſtarts a new Thought;

The Book has a Charm in't, the Book is in Fau't!

I ſhrewdly ſuſpect why the Book is to blame;

Alas! it has put Mr *Ivy* to ſhame

Puts him to the Bluſh and he now does deſpair,

His Blood will ne'er ſettle without *Iriſh* Air.

" Pray do me the Favour (ſaid he t'other Day,)

" This Book to the Owner, with Thanks, to convey;

" But who was the Author, or who was the Prince,

" I know not ; yet gueſs they are rotten long
  ſince.

" Had he wrote in her Time (as I am her Debtor,)

" I'd ſwear that he was your *Maria*'s Preceptor.

          To

To Mrs WHITMORE *on the Death of her Son.*

Written at Thurſtaſton, Jan. 16, 1731.

IN vain I ſeek to counſel or perſuade;
In vain with thee lament the much-lov'd Dead;
In vain with thine my ſwelling Sorrows flow,
In vain I Labour to appeaſe thy Woe:
Yet ſtill thou bid'ſt me write! Ah! poor Relief!
'Twill vent my own, but not aſſuage thy Grief.
With pleaſing Views of Bliſs ourſelves we cheat,
And our fond Paſſions favour the Deceit;
Vain Hope a moſt enchanting Scene diſplays,
And Love ne'er promiſes but happy Days.
On theſe alluring Proſpects eager bent,
We fondly this Side *Jordan* pitch our Tent.

Illuſive

Illusive Views! and Expectations vain !
Strait Disappointment and the ghastly Train
Of Life-corroding Grief, and baneful Care,
And a whole Troop of human Ills appear.

'Tis thus unerring Wisdom thinks it best,
To prove that Here, we shou'd not fix our Rest.
He grieves not willingly the human Race,
Afflictions oft are Tenders of his Grace
In Mercy he corrects, and wou'd controul
The darling Sin that most besets the Soul.
Our God a holy Jealousy avows,
And of no Creature rival Love allows
If ought on Earth too ardently we prize,
The much-lov'd Blessings vanish from our Eyes.
If here alone we fix our Home, and Care,
Reflect, no Mis'ry can with ours compare ·
But we beyond this Life our Hope extend ;
There, cast thy Anchor, dear afflicted Friend,

D d   There,

There our fure Hope, our certain Comfort lies ;

There God fhall wipe all Sorrow from our Eyes;

There thou fhall't meet thy much lamented Son,

In Virtue's Paths the Race of Life who run .

Whom Heav'n, in Mercy, to himfelf has chofe,

And refcued from a World of Sin and Woes·

He only knew the pleafant Morn of Life,

Nor felt the Pangs of Grief, or Storms of Strife.

No tort'ring Paffion difcompos'd his Breaft,

Peaceful he liv'd, and calmly funk to Reft.

At Heav'n's Decree, my Friend, no more repine,

But to th' Almighty's Will, thy own refign;

Ceafe vain Laments, and thefe diftracting Fears,

Supprefs thy Sighs, and dry thy fruitlefs Tears:

Submit with Rev'rence to th' inflicting Rod,

And own the Hand of an Almighty God.

J. B.

DECORUM.

DECORUM:

OR THE

FEMALE DEBATE.

Written in the Year 1739, *at the Desire of a Friend.*

"BEYOND the fix'd and settl'd Rules
  " Of Vice and Virtue in the Schools;

" Beyond the Letter of the Law,

" Which keeps out Men and Maids in Awe,

" The better Sort should set before 'em

" A Grace, a Manner, a Decorum ;

" Something that gives their Acts a Light,

" Makes 'em not only just, but bright ,

" And sets 'em in that open Fame,

" Which witty Malice cannot blame.

D d 2   " Thus

Thus PRIOR fung——fo far, fo good:
Yet this fine Leffon rais'd ill Blood !
So MYRA found, who, as a Friend,
Decorum fain would recommend.
The beauteous Lines above fhe chofe
As more affective far than Profe.
Advice, fhe thought, muft needs perfuade,
When in delightful Verfe convey'd.

" But, cries young CELIA, in a Paffion,
" Formality is out of Fafhion ,
" And what's Decorum ?——but the fame ?
" It differs only in the Name.
" The Modifh, and Genteel atteft
" A free Behaviour is the beft.
" But, if you PRIOR's Text maintain,
" What *his* Decorum is, explain.

His

His Senfe is clear in ev'ry Line,
Nor Comment needs to make it fhine ;
—Explain on what great PRIOR writ !—
Hard Task !—but CELIA, I fubmit.

Decorum is the Child of Reafon,
Obferving Order, Place, and Seafon ;
To Virtue, her undoubted Mother,
So like, we fcarce know one from t'other.
As round the Sun his Glories ftream,
Virtue emits this radiant Beam.

The Rough and Rigid, fay the Wife,
Should to the Graces facrifice;
To be both ftrictly juft and chafte;
Yet ftill, not with Decorum grac'd,
Is like the Diamond from the Mine,
Before the Polifh gives the Shine.

T' illuftrate

T' illuſtrate what I lay before ye,
Permit me to recite a Story.

" Agree'd ; oblige us with the Tale !
" If ſhort, to pleaſe, it cannot fail."

A Country Lady well I knew,
With Virtue bleſt, Good-breeding too ;
Tho' with the Poliſh'd more delighted,
She, Virtue in the rough, ne'er ſlighted.
The home-bred Houſe-wives often came,
And waited on the courteous Dame :
One Day, a plain, but honeſt Neighbour,
Who liv'd on Induſtry and Labour,
And ſerv'd her Houſehold, in his Way,
Invited was a while to ſtay
He took the Lady at her Word ;
—An unbred Female made the Third.
The Lady talk'd, what ſhe thought beſt
T' inſtruct, and pleaſe her humble Gueſt.

When enter Vifitants polite ;

The Ruftic ftrait withdraws from Sight ·

The Lady and her Friends agree

T' admit him of the Company ;

The Invitation is repeated,

Again, to his Content, he's feated ·

Again is faften'd by the Ears,

And charm'd with all he fees, and hears.

" But thefe fame Vifitants—were they

" Ladies, or Gentlemen, I pray ?

Both, CELIA, in that Circle met ;

Tho' not one Foppling, or Coquet.

All their Difcourfe fhould I recite,

'Twould wear out CELIA's Patience quite ;

It fhall fuffice me then to fay,

The Ruftics homeward took their Way.

' Neighbour ! cries he, d'ye mind how thefe,

' At once, can both inftruct, and pleafe.

'—How

'—How their Difcourfes ours excel !—

'—Their Words, like Dew on *Hermon*, fell :

' Their Virtue makes a goodly Show,

' In all they fpeak, and all they do!

' But you, and I, tho' juft, and true,

' Our Merit cannot fet to View.

' Our Virtue is too rough ; and many

' From thence, may think we have not any.

Thus, in Decorum, Virtue fhines,

And e'en th' untutor'd Mind refines!

And thus, infpires as juft a Thought,

As TULLY penn'd, or PLATO taught!

A Tale is eafier told, I find,

Than what you, CELIA, firft enjoyn'd ;

Tho' I Decorum would maintain,

Its Nature I can't well explain.*

But

* Decorum is that Becomingnefs, or Finefs of Behaviour, which is in
its Nature fo clofely united and riveted to Virtue, that there is no way of
feparating them ——The Difference between them is fo very fmall, that we
can better conceive what Decorum is, than explain it
   Tully's Offices, Book the Firft

But fure! howe'er it is defin'd,
It fprings from Rectitude of Mind,
Which gives an Elegance, a Grace ;
As Health Complexion to a Face.

" Can Woman rife to this Degree ?
" One Inftance, MYRA, let me fee:
—Yes,—in MARIA, you may trace
All that adorns the Female Race;
She, good and great, wife and polite,
Determines, fpeaks and acts aright :
Decorum in her Conduct lives,
To all her Actions Luftre gives.

The Great, who Virtue's Rules regard,
Should check the Bad, the Good reward,
Nor let high Titles fcreen the Dame,
Whofe Conduct ftains her noble Name ;
While fuch they equally prefer,
They act quite out of Character.

The

The Virtuous, in each Rank, fhould be
Obfervers of ftrict Decency;
Due Honours to the Worthy pay,
But fhun th' unthinking madly Gay.

If thus Decorum were maintain'd,
Vice would perceive itfelf difdain'd;
The Fear of public Scorn would awe,
Beyond the Rigour of the Law,
Beyond what Moralifts can teach;
Beyond ev'n what Divines can preach.

THALESTRIS heard all this with Scorn.
Such Lectures are not to be born!
She taps her Box, and fneering cries,
Some Folks are moft feverely wife!
But their fine Rules are oft neglected
By *fome* for Manners, much refpected.

The courtly FLORIO, whofe Addrefs

His very Rivals muft confefs;

He, who amid the Fair prefides,

The Mirth, the Dance, the Mufic guides:

Sure, he Decorum knows full well!

Yet fingled out the kindeft Belle;

What tho' her Honour had a Flaw!

He did not value that a Straw.

'Tis true, fome formal Ladies rag'd,

That fhe fhould be the firft engag'd;

Thefe in the Dance refus'd to joyn.

—Their Pride was ftiffer far than Mine!—

Were fuch, as pow'rful, as fevere,

They'd raife an Inquifition here,

All harmlefs Freedoms to abolifh,

And ev'ry Thing that's gay demolifh.

Their rigid Notions who can bear?

—'Tis peevifh Prudery all—I fwear.

I hate this rude cenforious Way;

What is't to me, who goes aftray?

I've

I've too much Manners to arraign

VANELIA, or her am'rous Train ;

T' impeach his Lordſhip, or his Grace,

Is Spleen, Ill-nature,—all Grimace!

I'll joyn in no ſuch rude Proceeding ;

—All *this* I take to be Good-breeding :

This ſure ! the Manner, the Decorum,

The better Sort ſhould ſet before 'em

What learn we now from this Debate?

—That Vice will have its Advocate.

That FLORIO, poliſh'd FLORIO ! choſe

The Weed, before the ſweeteſt Roſe.

That Prudence which, in Heathen Time,

Was own'd a Virtue moſt ſublime;

That Honour, and each moral Grace,

Now paſs for Prudery, Pride, Grimace.

To ſhun a wild, unworthy Creature,

Is Spleen, Ill-manners, and Ill-nature;

To blame, tho' juftly, is the Height
Of Envy, Jealoufy, and Spite.

  But maugre all THALESTRIS faid,
Chafte Virtue ftill uprears her Head ;
The Form of bright AUGUSTA wears,
And in four *Royal Nymphs* appears :
Their great Example fhall prevail,
When Argument, and Precept fail :
They, chief in Virtue, Rank, and Name,
Shall lead the Way to deathlefs Fame.

Mrs

‡‡

Some Poems which follow were written by other Hands ; but it was thought proper to re-print them here from the Gentleman's Magazine, as they gave Occasion to those signed MELISSA *in the Controversy with* FIDELIA, FIDO, &c. *which so agreeably entertained the Public in the Years* 1734 *and* 1735.

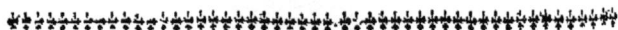

‡‡‡

To the Gentleman *who offer'd* 50
*Pounds to any Perfon who fhould write
the beft* P O E M *by* May *next on five
Subjects, viz.* Life, Death, Judgment, Heaven *and* Hell.

From the Gentleman's Magazine, July 1734.

BUT fifty Pounds!—A forry Sum!
   You'd more need offer half a *Plumb* :

Five weighty Subjects well to handle ?

Sir, you forget the Price of Candle ;

And Leather too; when late and foon,

I fhall be paceing o'er my Room,

Bite clofe my Nails, and fcratch my Head,

When other People are in Bed.

'Tis known old *Swift, Dan Pope* and *Young,*

Thofe Leaders of the rhiming Throng,

Arc

Are better paid for Meditations,

On the moft trifling Occafions;

The *Broomftick, Benefit of Fa—ing* ;

Or any Whim they fhew their Art in.

Alas, an idle Farce, or Play,

Such as TOM THUMB, or *Phillida,*

Is better lik'd, will fooner fell,

Than pious Subjeƈts treated well.

I ever lov'd the true Sublime,

And think the Theme is worth my Time ;

But I'm a Maid, whofe Fortune's fmall,

Or I would ask no Pay at all.

But ftraight fit down, invoke my Mufe;

For thofe are Subjeƈts I would chufe.

But as an Author lately writ,

The Mufes' they are Virgins yet ;

And may be,—till they Portions get:

So, as 'tis Wealth that all Men follow,

Not *Jove*'s fair Daughters, nor *Apollo* :

Methinks,

Methinks, I'd fain increase the Blessing,

For which such Crowds are daily pressing.

O Wealth! thou *universal Passion*!

So much desir'd in this our Nation;

That should the Doctor write again,

He would say *Wealth* instead of *Fame*.

But to return from my Digression,

And be more clear in my Expression;

That is, Sir, if you'd have it done,

Pray add a Cypher to your Sum.

I did but jest 'bout half a *Plumb*.

Lincoln, *Sept.* 23, 1734.   FIDELIA.

Another by the same.

From the Gentleman's *Magazine* for *November* 1734.

INDEED, Mr URBAN, I must tell you, 'tis hard

That you, to my Poem, should shew no Regard;

You might have said something, had it been the less :

But to send no Return, but my own, from the Press,

F f   Makes

Makes me almoſt wiſh I had kept to my Stitching.

But this Scribling's a Thing ſo confounded bewitching!

Perhaps, by my Raillery, you might opine,

I could not expatiate on Subjects Divine:

But that is raſh Judging; I'll warrant the Dean

In his Time has made Sermons,—you know who I

     mean ;—

Not that I ſpeak this by way of Reflection,

For I love the Dean with the utmoſt Affection ;

I'm charm'd with his Writings, I admire his brave

     Spirit,

That dares to diſtinguiſh 'twixt Grandeur and Merit;

And you may inform him I gladly would take him

For better for worſe, all others forſaking ;

You may add, that I love him to ſuch a Degree,

I ſhould be content to croſs over the Sea,

That *Vaneſſa*, that favourite of *Vulcan*'s fair Dame,

For her dear *Cadenus* ne'er felt ſuch a Flame ;

That

That my Paſſion's ſo great, I can't live without him;

That he's more need than ever of a Help-meet about him;

Oh! how was I griev'd when I read it laſt Poſt,

That he had the Senſe of his Hearing quite loſt!

I pray'd *Jove* from all other Ills to defend him,

And long'd to be with him, that I might attend him;

Then would I ſo nurſe him, and make ſuch a Bride,

He ſhould never once wiſh that the Knot was unty'd;

For ſo good a Wife I ſhould certainly be,

Ought diſpleaſing to him wou'd be hateful to me·

The Example of thoſe he diſlikes I'd avoid,

And imitate *Stella*, and Miſs *Biddy Floyd*.

So, good Mr *Urban*, when you draw this Petition,

Intreat him to pity my heartleſs Condition;

And then for your Prizes your Poets may ſhift,

I ſhall have all I wiſh, when I get Doctor *Sw —t.*

FIDELIA.

To

❀❀❀❀❀❀❀❀❀❀❀❀❀❀❀❀❀❀❀❀❀❀❀❀❀❀❀❀❀❀

To FIDELIA *in Anſwer to her two*
EPISTLES.

BRIGHT Maid! ſince URBAN you accuſe
    That no Regard is paid your Muſe,
And at his wonted Silence vex,
(A hateful Penance to your Sex,)
Leſt this miſconſtru'd Slight t oMerit
So prompt a Genius ſhou'd diſpirit,
He fears, looks careful, rubbs his Sconſe,
And begs ſome Friend wou'd make Reſponſe—
I wait to ſerve him at a Whiſtle.
Muſe!——write the Lady an Epiſtle.

You own quite thro' your amorous Paper
A Paſſion for th' *Hibernian* Draper,
Tho' yet (beneath the Roſe we ſpeak)
You call'd him *Old*, but t'other Week.

But

But *Mum*—we fcorn your Words to catch—
Befides, you pray we'd help the Match:
We'd gladly in your Service lift,
Dear Nymph——but fear——we can't affift.
Your Perfon you conceal-——the Dean
We 're not fo happy to have feen ;
Wou'd you have put us in Condition
To recommend you by Petition,
You fhou'd have given us plain Direction,
Your Temper, Stature, Age, Complexion,—
'Tis plain you've Wit ; we own it fhines,
With obvious Beauty, in your Lines,
Squire WORTHY too Encom'ums fends
That muft be good which he commends.

   The Dean within a Poft or two
Will fee in Print your Billet-doux,
And——let's fuppofe he fhou'd confent,
Do none their Marriage Choice repent ?

To ferve and honour, will it fuit you ?

Have you well weigh'd that trying Duty ?

Oft Wives (and Miftreffes of Rank)

Have play'd their Sovereigns many a Prank,

Afpir'd to govern in their Houfes,

And made meer Vaffals of their Spoufes.

Thus the foft Pad, a gentle Titt,

A while bears tame the ambling Citt ;

But, pamper'd, wou'd he then beftride her,

She bounces, frisks, and flings her Rider.

You promife fair, for Nurfe or Wife,

And wifely judge the married Life

Wou'd more than ever prove endearing,

Since the good Dean has loft his hearing.

A pleafing Calm, well fuited Station.—

I'm Deaf—and know it by Probation.

But oh!—the Prize—I'm bid acquaint you,

Is rais'd—yet fear 'twill difappoint you,

From

From *5* we blot the Cypher nigh,   *50*

And place his fair twin Figure by,   *55*

No matter—you, Satiric Scoffer,

Scorn *50* Pounds, a paltry Offer,

You give the Poets Leave to *fhift*

For fordid Gold—your Bait's a *Swift*;

He'll tempt, it feems, when nothing can.

Well—I'll Addrefs the holy Man.

   " For Female Wits (they're not a few)

   " Propofe—YOUR-SELF—good Doctor do;

   " That Prize will fure be moft inviting—

   " You'll fet the Women all on Writing.

ASTROPHIL.

FIDELIA *to* SYLVANUS URBAN.

From the *Magazine* for *March* 1735.

I Waited twice two Months, to fee
If my dear Dean would anfwer me;

I knew

I knew old Men were not, like young,

Hafty to anfwer right or wrong;

They're wary, and deliberate long.

Nay, loth to think he'd prove unkind,

I laid the Fault on Waves or Wind;

But fince he ftill continues Mum,

Alas! not only Deaf—but Dumb;

What fhould I do—but give him over,

And chufe at Home fome kinder Lover.

For I have Billet-doux each Morning,

To beg I wou'd reject and fcorn him ,

JACK RESTLESS fues in humble Plight,

TOM SPRIGHTLY does in Raptures write;

And to exprefs how great their Flames,

They call the Doctor ugly Names.

But be this known unto them all,

I love him fo—and ever fhall,

That whoe'er hopes to gain my Favour,

Muft not fpeak Ill of him however:

And as to what he wrote not long fince,

Of Female * Minds, upon my Confcience,

To think it general—would be Nonfenfe.

'Tis like he meant fome certain Dame,

Who falfely had afpers'd his Fame;

And he to be reveng'd on her,

Writes thus at large her Character :

I vow I'm not offended by it,

Let fhe it reprefents apply it.

Jove never gave fo large a Share

Of Wit, to ridicule the Fair.

No, fure he wrote for fome good End,

As a weak Sifter's Fault to mend.

We know the Doctor's well inclin'd,

And would reform all human Kind;

Which he attempts in fuch a Way,

So new, fo witty, and fo gay,

That while he chides he pleafes too;

A Secret known to very few.

G g

But

* *See* Furniture of a Woman's Mind, By Dr *Swift* Gent. *Mag. Vol V.*

But—since I can't obtain his Favour,

Quite to forget him I'll endeavour,

So Farewell, cruel Dean! for ever.

   Linc. March 15.   FIDELIA.

✳✳✳✳✳✳✳✳✳✳ ✳✳✳✳✳✳ '✳✳✳✳ ✳✳✳✳ ✳✳✳✳✳✳✳✳

MELISSA *to* FIDELIA.

From the *Magazine* for *April* 1735.

*F*IDELIA, I find, a Retinue of Poets,

   From the higheſt Claſs, quite down to the low

      Wits ;

From *Apollo*'s true Sons, to his vain Implorers,

Moſt humbly profeſs themſelves your Adorers

Friend *Urban*'s judicious,—he gives but the * Name

Of *ſuch*, whoſe Encomiums are *Smoak* and no *Flame*,

Tho' their Panegyricks, he reckons but Lumber,

Yet their Names, Cypher-like, may mount up the

      Number.

                            I hope,

* See *Magazine* Vol. V. p 155, Note 1

I hope, dear *Fidelia*, as loyal, as witty,

Nor doubt I the leaft, but you're youthful and pretty,

If Quarrels fhou'd rife with *the Don*, or *Monfieur*,

Will engage each Admirer to go *Volunteer*.

A Company foon, I believe, you cou'd raife

To fight for the King, and to fing in your Praife ;

And fure, greatExploits they'd perform,—if they *fight*,

With but half the Spirit, with which you can *write*.

Like *Pallas*, the Goddefs of Arms and of Arts,

At once you'll infpire both their Heads and their
     Hearts.

Your *Genius* appears too in fome of their Lays,

And the *Rivals grown friendly unite in your Praife,

For in your fweet Numbers, are fuch potent Charms,

Shou'd *you* once command 'em—they'll all rufh to
     Arms.

So *Græcian Corinna* infpir'd Old and Young,

And her Country was fav'd, by the Force of her Song.

? See *Gent Mag* Vol. V. p. 155 Poems and Notes in Col 1.

Songs, Odes, and Epiftles, I've wrote,——and
    what not !

And ventur'd amongft the *Male Bards* to the Grot;

And once I defign'd to have try'd on the *Theme*

Propos'd by *Sylvanus* for *Pounds* and for *Fame*;

But foon as *Fidelia*'s bright *Genius* was feen

Set off, and applauded in his *Magazine*;

I then recollected, what often I'd read,

That *Pallas* proceeded from *Jupiter*'s Head.

'Tis a parallel Cafe—I fufpect—by his Leave,

That *Fidy*, like *Sybil*, fpeaks out of a CAVE.

Be that as it will;—'tis to me very plain,

She'll win *Fifty Pounds*,—tho' fhe lofes the *Dean.*

MELISSA.

Anfwer

Answer to the foregoing, by a Gentleman who signed FIDO, *and saw all* MELISSA*'s before they were sent to the Press.*

From the *Magazine* for *May* 1735

FOR your Epistle—smart, obliging Dame,
(Unknown your real, or poetick Name.)
I, dear *Fidelia*'s Friend—her Lover too,
Without her Leave address these Lines to you.

The *injur'd Fair One,* living above Ground,
Sends from no *hollow* CAVE an artful Sound.
No *Goddess* born of JOVE's all-teeming Brain,
But Flesh and Blood—of true poetick Strain.
Nor call'd like *Helen* on the Stage in *Drury* :—
—For CAVE's no Conjurer—I can assure ye.

Let *Monsieur,* or the *Don,* or *both* advance ;
From her no Succours against *Spain,* or *France.*

Our

Our *Ministers* will make th' *Allies* to shake,
And as they brew (*themselves*) so let them bake!
Most of her wheedling, servile, rhiming Crew
For *Fire* and *Spirit* are oblig'd to you.
'Tis true, *Fidelia* has the Knack to write;
Not so, perhaps, her *Scriblers* how to fight:
And since the Dean's *not only deaf,* but—*dumb,*
I have some Hopes of her myself—but *Mum*!

Who traffick not in Truth,—will soon believe
That others deal in Falsehood, and deceive :
As all seems Yellow to the jaundic'd Eye,
As you may think 'tis CAVE that writes—not I.
Fair are his *Terms,* and *open* to the *Croud,*
You catch at JUNO—not an empty *Cloud.*

Safe—for *Fidelia*—safe! attempt the *Prize*;
Wound with your Pen (whatever with your Eyes)

LIFE, JUDGMENT, HEAV'N, and HELL—and hear
   the Call

Of *fifty Pounds*—much louder than 'em all !

Each Subject grand, as grand *Augusta's* Street !

Yet trod as oft' by mean poetick Feet.

And since DEATH favours neither High, nor Low,

Let Low, no more than High, forbear the Foe :

Vindictive follow with avenging Breath,

And never leave 'till they have *murder'd* DEATH.

                      FIDO.

To the unknown M--------A, *on her Epi-*
stle to FIDELIA.

MADAM,

IF *Fidelia's* gay Wit was the Child of my Brain,
   As you seem to suspect in your smart courtly
      Strain ;

                     Tho'

Tho' you Honour me much by the wild Imputation,

Yet my *Heart* were at Stake for my *Head*'s Reputation.

Tho' *hollow*—and *founding*—are Terms for a *Cave*,

I'm too *empty* for *all this Fineſſe* of a Knave ;

And had rather (believe me) be thought a mere

    Dunce,

Than forfeit my Fame, and my Int'reſt at once :

Songs, Odes, and Epiſtles you've wrote,—and what

    not !

And ventur'd amongſt the Male Bards *to the Grot* ,

Pray, how was the Weather—cold—temp'rate or

    hot ?

Scarce ought, but the Gout, my Eaſe is a Curb on,

Save how with Applauſe to acquit Mr *Urban,*

By Judges as learn'd as the Heads of the *Sorbonne.*

Then, tho' *Fidy* ſhou'd write—you'll have Juſtice

    from me,

If they ſhall adjudge—you write better than ſhe.

                      E. C.

FIDELIA *to* MELISSA.

TO you, MELISSA, worthy Friend,
    FIDELIA does this Greeting send :
Whereas you've on *Parnassus* been,
And all the Sons of Fame have seen,
Ventur'd that lofty Hill to climb,
Which cost, no doubt, much Pains and Time,
And kindly sent me News from thence,
How they all feel my Influence ;
So far that not one single Heart,
From High to Low, has scap'd my Dart :
—Know—I'm a Nymph of no mean Spirit,
And will reward you for your Merit ;
So, pray, mount *Pegasus* again,
And meet once more the shining Train,
In gentle Numbers let 'em know
That I compassionate their Woe ;

But,

But, since I must not have the Dean,

I ne'er can think of Love again;

So look on all as coldly now,

As *Dido*, in the Shades below,

When she the *Trojan* Hero saw.

Say then—I freely do resign

Them all to be intirely thine:

Yet don't be vain, tho' you have Charms,

Nor think of sending them to Arms;

For if you do, they must retreat,

Or be most scandalously beat;

Since, as to fighting for the King,

Without their Hearts, there's no such Thing:

So be advis'd, my dearest Creature,

In all you do, to show good Nature;

Nor let Suspicions thee perplex,

I feign my Name, but not my Sex.

FIDELIA.

MELISSA

✿✿✿✿✿✿✿✿✿✿✿✿✿✿✿✿✿

MELISSA *to* FIDO.

From the *Magazine* for *June* 1735.

TO gallant *Fido*, Peace I meekly fend;
 Peace to *Fidelia's Lover*, and her *Friend.*
Friend I'm to *all* whofe *Senfe* or *Wit* excel,
Flow they from *Hippocrene*, or *Clerkenwell.*

Your *Miftrefs* bids me, in a peccant Strain,
To mount the *winged Steed* and meet—*her Train* '
—For *Lovers*, let diftreffed Damfels roam,
Who cannot find, or *Choice*, or *Cheap*, at Home.
Of all *her wheedling, fervile, rhiming Crew,*
I do proteft, I can admire but *you.*
—Thanks—tho' I can't except her bounteous *Gift*;
I wifh 'twere in my *Pow'r* to give her *Swift.*
—Wifh *he'd* reward a *Love* fo true, fo pure .
And in Return—fhe cou'd his *Deafnefs* cure.

My

My *Pegasus*, tho' fleet, oppress'd with Weight,
Wou'd ne'er attempt *Parnassus'* lofty Height :
At awful Distance, I the *Summit* view,
  Admiring POPE and SWIFT, YOUNG, HARTE, and
    — You !
For *Pinks*, and *Heart's-ease*, I the *Borders* rove,
To gather Wreaths for *Friendship*, or for *Love*.
Tho' unambitious high'r to climb the *Steep* ;
Yet from the very *Flat*, I'd gladly keep.
For *there* no grateful *Flow'rs* their Odours blow ;
But Crops of *Poppies* in full Plenty grow :
And harmless *Simples* for *Fidelia's* Garland :
—Tho' *Sylvius'* Chaplet sprung not in that bare Land,
Sylvius, you'll own, ascends the *Hill* with Ease ,
And chaunts out Numbers which your *Mistress* please.

If *Fidy's* former Lines spoke *manly Sense*,
In my Esteem ;—must that give you Offence ?

If

If for our *Sex* I thought her *Wit* uncommon ;

Muſt you degrade her quite to—very Woman ?

Meer *Fleſh* and *Blood*—and vaunting *whiſper* me ?

That you've ſome Hopes, Bone of your Bone ſhe'll be?

—But ſhe's all *Spirit* ;—and you're much to blame ;

What !—gallant *Fido* boaſting '—fie, for ſhame !

—Beſides all this, ſhe'll certainly reſent

Your chuſing *me* to be your *Confident.*

Sh' has ſilenc'd me—ſhou'd ſhe ſend you a *Gag?*

The expreſſive *Mum* you ſent in truſty *Mag,*

I apprehend.—but ſhe the *Boaſt* will catch ;

And then, ſmart *Fido,* you may meet your *Match!*

But, why ſo witty on my Eyes—I pray ?

—You'd give a *Groat,*—to ſee 'em, I dare ſay.

You can't believe what Havock *they* have made ;

—The little *Rogues* ſtill lurk in *Ambuſcade.*

No haughty Strains I to *Fidelia* penn'd ;

If *feign'd,* or *real* ſhe, I ſpoke the *Friend.*

If

If *real*; to her *Wit*, Applaufe I fent,

(I own, 'twas not a *Lover*'s Compliment)

Ev'n my *Sufpicions* muft her Glory raife;

T' afcribe her Lines to C—v e, was higheft Praife.

If this, *th' applauded Fair* won't eafy make ;

On me, let the dear Creature, Vengeance take.

Unvex'd with *Spleen*, unpractis'd in *Deceit*;

I frankly wrote what Numbers us'd to prate :

From my blunt *Pen* foft *Strokes*, not *Wounds*, arife;

Soft as *its Feather*—harmlefs as my *Eyes*.

No Colouring it wears of Jaundice Hue ;

Meant no Affront to *Cave*, means none to *you*.

Defenfive now, I ufe *it* as a Shield;

For, *Sir*, a *Briton* knows not how to yield.

Unknown my real, and poetick Name ;

Pray, *Fido*, do not lafh me into *Fame*.

MELISSA

MELISSA *to Mr* E. C.

SIR I'm concern'd your *Heart* fhould lie at *Stake;*
    Concern'd, my Words fhou'd ill Impreffions
      make.

Since on your *Probity*, no *flur* defign'd;

On th' *Imputation*, you've too much refin'd.

In merry mood, my Fancy join'd wild Rumour,

With no Defign to vent, or raife *ill Humour*.

—Suppofe a *Stroke* of fome fmall *Weight* was gi-
     ven ;

Sure *three* to *one*, muft make the *Balance* even!

For Shame it were, and wou'd quite fpoil your Vannt-
     ing ;

The *three* now *weigh'd* ,—if *they* fhould be—*found*
     wanting.

The

The *Gout* is not fevere,—since you're so merry,
To *rámble* from your *Way* with waggish *Query.*
—*Temp'rate the Weather was,* and *cool* the Grot:
Therefore, I wonder much, a *Cave's* so *hot.*
No *Conjurer,* quoth *Fido*;—yet how ready
You *jingo'd!*—and then strait pops up the Lady !
Who to *Melissa* sings a *lofty Lay*:
—But to *rais'd Spirits,* I dare little say.
Her *Air,* and *Ditty* both, your *Head* acquit ;
'Twas *Spleen,* not *Brain,* produc'd that *puny Wit.*

❁❁❁❁❁❁❁❁❁❁❁❁❁❁❁❁❁❁❁❁❁❁❁❁❁❁

Tantæne Animis cœlestibus Iræ?

FIDELIA and MELISSA Quarrel !
Sure, 'tis not which shou'd wear the Laurel.
They're each so well deserving Praise,
We wish they wou'd divide the Bays.

Is either wounded? Heav'ns forbid it,
And petrify the Ink that did it.

But what gigantick Mufe durft fly
To ftorm againft the brighter Sky?
Contending Goddeffes wou'd yield,
And to thefe Females quit the Field.
Why then fuch Jars? are they grown jealous?
No—there are num'rous pretty Fellows
    Can court in Verfe, in Verfe betroth,
    Willing to gratify them both.

But yet the *Dean* may prove a Foil,
And all our fubtle Thoughts beguile;
Behind his Name another lurk,
That might indeed make woful Work;
For of all Plagues wherewith we're curft,
Sure that of Rivals is the worft.

By

By Solitude our Pains encreafe,

By Partners we Afflictions eafe;

In Love alone we fullen grow,

And hate Companions of our *Woe*:

But where's the *Phaon* cou'd engage,

And charm two *Sapho*'s in one Age?

S. U.

MELISSA's *Anfwer to the Verfes fign'd* S. U.

From the *Magazine* for *July* 1735.

MELISSA with FIDELIA quarrel'
       Not for the *Penfion* with the *Laurel*!

Colly wou'd make a woful Pother,

Eie *he'd* relinquifh *one* or *t'other*·

But cou'd the *Laurel* add a *Grace*

And *Air*, becoming, to my *Face*?

Ah!

Ah! no:—I'm certain, could I win *it*,

I'd make a hideous Figure in *it*.

Facetious *Fido* wou'd defpife

My empty *Crown* and hollow *Eyes*·

Perhaps he'd trip to antient *Rome*,

To prove *Meliffa* paft her *Bloom*;

With far-fetch'd *Smiles* wou'd teaze her,

And cry,—fhe's *cunning*—as old *Cæfar*;

Who *flily*, as the Story fays,

To hide his *Baldnefs*, wore the *Bays*.

Whence *Fido* might pretend to fay,

My *Head* was either *bald* or *grey*.

Alas!—my *Pate* fhou'd ne'er have Reft;

My *Laurel* too, become a Jeft—

—I'll be contented in my *Pinner*,

Let bright *Fidelia* be the *Winner*!

Tho' *Daphne* from *Apollo* fled;

With Joy fhe'll deck *Fidelia*'s Head.

If fhe deferves *it*——I declare it,

I wifh her Life, and Health, to wear *it*.

Nor

Nor am I, in the leaft, grown jealous
For *Phaons*, or fuch pretty Fellows.
Nay,—I'll not quarrel for *Decanus*;
Our Conteft is for you, *Sylvanus*,
Who now, like *Britain*, hold the *Scale*,
Left either *Side* too much prevail.
—But, Sir, you've * faid, *my Pen's too keen*,
In fath'ring *Fidy's* Wit on *Spleen*.
My *Mufe* here offers to maintain,
That *Spleen* infpires, as well as *Brain*.

In *Prior's Alma*, pleafe to look,
You'll find, I talk not without *Book*.
That *Bard* does logically fing,
The *Spleen's* a wond'rous *ufeful* Thing.
" Elfe we fhou'd want both *Gibe* and *Satir*;
" And all be *burft* with pure *Good-nature*."

In

---

* In a private Letter to another Correfpondent.

In meek *Religion's* Caufe, 'tis not
Alone, the *Sanguin* and the *Hot*;
But e'en the *Mild,* and eke the *Cold,*
Rather than *burft*, have chofe to *fcold.*
O, let the *Britifh* MARO tell,
Can Wrath in Heav'nly Bofoms dwell!
Divinity fpit Fire ! fo Keen !
—*Urban* ! infure thy *Magazine.*—

Was not his Grace of *Buckingham,*
Of *Prior's* Mind; or much the fame ?
His *Effay* read—You'll find the *Page*—
" *Mac Flecno* was the Child of *Rage.*

A greater *Name* I can produce ;
Will *Pope* forgive the daring Mufe ?
'Twas either POPE, or PHOEBUS writ,
" That *Spleen's* the Sire of Female Wit.

One Inftance more, which ferves me beft,
And will demonftrate all the Reft :
If 'twas the *Theme* that did infpire
Poetick Energy and Fire;
* Indulgent *Spleen*, to *Thee* we owe
The brighteft Piece our *Sex* can fhow.
At FINCH's *Tomb* be Honours pay'd;
And endlefs Blifs attend her *Shade.*

For me,—fincerely, 'tis confeft,
He feldom deigns to be my *Gueft;*
Stays but a Minute, now-and-then,
When much provok'd, to point my *Pen.*

FIDELIA's Charge I can't fuftain;
She's doubly arm'd with *Spleen* and *Brain.*
Let *this* or *that*, infpire her *Lays,*
MELISSA yields to her the *Bays.*

FIDO

* *Spleen,* a Poem, by the Countefs of *Winchelfea*

✠✠✠✠✠✠✠✠✠✠✠✠✠✠✠✠✠✠✠✠✠✠✠·✠·✠✠✠✠✠✠✠✠✠✠✠✠✠✠✠✠✠✠✠✠✠✠

FIDO *to* MELISSA.

From the *Magazine* for *July* 1735.

WHAT mighty Things from small Begin-
           nings rife!

MELISLA writes,—and C—VE and FIDO dies!

FIDELIA too but ftruggles with her Fate,

And may repent her Foolery too late.

  My great Offence was for my *Miftrefs'* fake ;

For both her *Mufe* and *Being* were at Stake.

Poor frantick C—VE bewail'd his dang'rous Wound;

And groan'd, and echo'd in a murm'ring Sound !

FIDELIA next, indignant at your Sneer,

Joyn'd our Militia—without Thought or Fear :

Yet what avail our Courage, and our Odds;

For what are *Pigmies* in the Hands of *Gods* !

                           Say,

Say, dreadful HEROINE ! *ambiguous Fair*!
What mean your Forces? Is it Peace, or War?
Peace you declare,—like the *Moſt Chriſtian King*,
Yet who believes he ever meant the Thing!
At leaſt 'tis plain you'd have us underſtand
That Peace is better made with Sword in Hand.
But hold—this Simile can never hit;
No! but the *German* will exactly fit:
Like his *Imperial Troops* you watch the Foe,
And *weak in Numbers* dare confront the Blow.
Go on to rally, and maintain the Field,
Nor let the *Briton* with the *Woman* yield.

Your Stratagems are not to War confin'd;
Some Strokes there are of a much ſofter kind.
Thank ye MELISSA!—But with FID in View,
'Twou'd be ſurpriſing I ſhou'd think of You.
I hear with Wonder of your conqu'ring Eyes!
(From you I hear ! and yet—no Wiſhes riſe.)

This

This certain Comfort you may take however,
I promise ye, I'll never *boaſt the Favour*.

Poorly you play a SYLVIUS or a SWIFT,
Love's laſt Contrivance---a mean Thread-bare Shift ,
One of your Plots (my Life on't!) will miſcarry,
I'm very ſure the DEAN will never marry ,
And as for SYLVIUS,---I'm not in much pain,
Alas, po r Poet ! he is not the Man.
So you, and he---invited by the Weather,
May fondly go a *ſimpling* both together :
Or ſpoil the Banks where Pinks and Lillies blow,
While Wreaths of Laurel for FIDELIA grow !
Nor fear your Fate, of being *very Flat*,
He'll like you ne'er a jot the worſe for that.

But e'er your Slaughter farther you extend,
Hear the pacific Treaty which I ſend.
Let but the Nuptials, I propoſe, be ſafe,
We'll ſoon get Heirs, ſhall make all *Europe* laugh,

K k   Scarce

Scare *high Parnaſſus* with a bold Defiance,

Weak, and unequal to the grand Alliance:

Io MELISSA ! *Io* SYLVIUS ! ring;

Io FIDELIA *' Io* FIDO ! ſing

FIDO.

MELISSA *to* FIDO.

From the *Magazine* for *Auguſt* 1735.

WHAT lurking *Venom* in my Gooſe-quill
lies !

' MELISSA writes—and C—VE and FIDO dies!

If FIDO dies, I can't the loſs ſuſtain,

I ne'er ſhall have *ſuch* Complements again.

Ne'er ſhall my *Eyes,* in bright *Encomiums,* ſhine,

Nor I be ſtyl'd the dreadful HEROINE '

Ne'er *weak in Numbers,* like the *German* rally,

Nor with the *Grand Allies,* at diſtance dally.

Oh!

Oh! I shall lose a thousand pretty *Things*,
Which now, to me, obliging FIDO sings.
'Twill make me hate, this *Homicide*, my *Pen*,
And almost vow,—I ne'er will write agen.

How can you, FIDO, thus a *Woman* slight!
Tax me with *Murther*,—scare me with your *Sprite*
Well; I'll forgive, since, you're *Alive* ; I find.
Long may you *Live*! tho' still to me unkind!

Your *dying* Strains, an *Elegy* bespoke ;
But Death, and Slaughter, you soon turn'd to Joke.
Of fierce Exploits you treat, like *French Ro-
mances* ;
Like *them* conclude, with sprightly nuptial *Fancies*.

I'm quite transported with your *lofty Phrase* ;
Io, MELISSA lives in FIDO's Lays.

Thus

Thus *Monks* of Yore the martial * ELFRED

prais'd;

knockt down *Heroes*, and who *Cities* rais'd.

— *Mer* ' and *dreadful Heroine* !

— *you as Alecto*, or *Medusa*, shine.

Ne'er may the crooked *Rib* dear FIDO vex,

Who pays such wond'rous Honours to the *Sex*

Wide, as his *Fame* extends, *mine* shall be spread,

Long as his *Name* shall live, *mine* will be read'

Ceafe your *Applause* '—left I too, haughty grow,

Applause had ill effect on—you know who

—And is what you inform me, really true?

And can't you think of me, while FID's in view?

FIDELIA's prefent, —were MELISSA fo;

You'd hardly like *her* worfe, than--now you do.

Pray

* OF fle'a *friens, O'er or Virgo curorum,*

O Eifeia pstrens, nurum digna Vir.

Holinfh B vi p 152

Pray think, ere you again my *Eyes* upbraid
Who made *Mars* bellow, but *the Blue-ey'd Maid*
Vain-glorious she '—methinks, I hear you cry,
The GODDESS *is my* FRIEND, *my beſt* ALLY.
—Be not too haſty—I'll not yield her ſo,—
To e'er a *haughty*, or *inſulting Foe*,
Th' imperial *Eagle* ſhall his *Plumes* extend,
And the PALLADIUM from your Force defend :
But if *he* fails;—a Stratagem I'll try,
Her fav'rite *Bird* ſhall whoot ye—'till you fly.

   The *French* and *Germans*, courtly and diſcreet,
Can with much Gallantry, each other greet.
And I, a gen'rous *Foe*, will promiſe *this*,
I'll ſcorn to take th' Advantage of my *Phiz*;
But keep my *Vizor* on, and *Diſtance* too,
—-Leſt my vindictive *Eyes*, ſhou'd pierce you
   through.

To *Wood*, or *Cave*, I ne'er a *Simpling* went,
But when the *Allies*, call'd for their *Complement*;
Nor, fhall I like to walk, where *Simples* grow;
Unlef., you call for *Hellebore*, or fo.
Let FIDY take the *Laurel Wreath* and *Fido*;
Know , I'm refolv'd, I ne'er will burn like *Dido*.

What is the *Grand Alliance* broke ?—I pray,
That fimply you fuftain the dreadful *Fray* ?
The *Donna*, and *Sardinian*, foon withdrew;
The *Gaul* with *Numbers*, ftill confronts my View,
His fierce Battalions marfhals once again;
And with his *Sable Troops* o'erfpreads the *Plain*.
Undaunted *Monfieur* capers o'er the *Field*,
Nor will the *Hero* to the *Heroine* yield.

So the renowned *Don*, *la Mancha*'s Knight,
Without or Fear, or Wit, would brave the Fight.

But yet—left *dreadful* HEROINE fhou'd beat ye—
You fend in *Mag*. O ftrange, *pacifick Treaty*!
Of this *your Treaty*, I ne'er heard 'till now,
Where, was it *held* ? by *whom*, and *when*, and *how?*
Preliminaries firft, fhou'd be agreed,
And *Place*, and *Time*, ere we to *treat* proceed
Then, let your *Plenipo*, aud *mine* appear;
And, in due *Form*, what you propofe,—I'll hear.

The Reafon's plain, why SYLVIUS you afperfe,
He charm'd your *Miftrefs* with enchanting Verfe.
And left he fhou'd a pow'rful *Rival* be,
With wily *Arts* you'd fheer him off, to me.
Of your *Propofal*, I can not allow;
For know,—I'm promis'd, and won't break my *vow*.
Tho' to the *Yoke*, I'll not, as yet, fubmit,
Nor yield to *marry*, 'till I have more Wit.
But fince for *Hymen's Chains*, you 're almoft giddy;
Pray give me leave, to wait on YOU, and FIDDY.

SYLVIUS

SYLVIUS and I, will *Partners be*, for once;

Call to *Crowdero*, for—*The Lad's a Dunce*.

Lead up that *Country-dance*—to grace your Wed-
    ding,

And wait to throw the *Stocking*, at your bedding.

Ring *Io* FIDO ' o'er your *Perecranium* ·

—Let the *great Laureat* fing, th' *Epithalanium*.

MELISSA *to* SYLVANUS URBAN.

IF, Sir, the Balance you pretend to hold,
    Why was grofs *Bullion* left in FIDO's *Gold*?

Had you his *Piece*, impartially furvey'd,

And its intrinfick worth, maturely weigh'd;

Your Judgment fure, wou'd ne'er have let it pafs,

Till, from the *Gold*, you had thrown out the BRASS

  Our Legiflators, yet, no law have made,

That Women fhou'd, in diff'rent *Coin*, be paid ·

                            But

But our licentious Wits, new Mints exp'ore,

Imprefs foul Images on *pureft Ore* ;

On candid *Words*, ftamp *Meanings* unrefin'd,

Becaufe they know, we can't repay in *Kind*.

Who vend falfe *Coin*, are purnifh'd for th' Of-
    fence;

Then why fhou'd URBAN with falfe *Wit* difpenfe ?

If with Applaufe, you wou'd yourfelf acquit,

Let not *bafe meanings* pafs like *fterling Wit*.

❀❀|❀❀❀❀❀❀❀❀❀❀❀❀|❀❀❀|❀❀❀❀❀❀❀❀❀❀❀

To MELISSA, *in Anfwer to the foregoing.*

From the fame *Magazine*

WHY, when *Antagonifts* the Fair offend,
    For their *bafe Meaning* will fhe chide her
    Friend ?

Who ne'er prefum'd the *Balance to fuftain*,

As her *fatiric Complement* would feign.

           L l   When

When from the Prefs your Letters you perufe
You blame, if but a *trivial Stop* you lofe.
Think—how the Wrong wou'd kindle *Fido*'s Rage,
Shou'd we expunge *whole Couplets* from his Page.

If you with Juftice urge our Laws confign
To penal Smart for vending fpurious Coin,
He'd urge, no doubt, the Crime a Statute further,
And, breathing Wrath, indict us for his Murther.

Forgive, *Meliffa*—Controverfial Wit
Our *equal Page* unalter'd fhou'd tranfmit.
Each bold Oppofer you can foil with Eafe,
As fure to conquer, as you're skill'd to pleafe.   S.U.

FIDO's *laſt Epiſtle to* MELISSA.

From the *Magazine* for *September* 1735

WELL !—'tis confeſs'd, I play'd the Lover,
 To give my Plot a ſpecious Cover :
But Jeſts apart—I vow 'tis true—
I neither burn for *Fid*, nor you.
The *eaſy Vein* in which ſhe writes,
And your more *learn'd*, judicious Flights,
May charm yourſelves, and pleaſe your Friends,
But Wives ſhou'd anſwer other Ends.

Ill wou'd the vain romantick Heart
Supply the Hus'wife's better Part.
—With *Medals* let the Curious ſhine,
Grant me, ye Gods ! Life's *current Coin*.

Wh

What! take a Woman to a Wife,
Who leads a wild, poetick Life!
—Give me the unaffected *Fair*,
Who makes a Family her Care,
With Wisdom suited to her Station,
To charm her *Spouse*—and not the *Nation*:
With Prudence blest—and, tho' no *Scribe*,
She's worth the whole *poetick Tribe*.

* * * * * * * * * *
* * * * * * * * * * *
* * * * * * * * * * *
* * * * * * * * * * *

Amongst yourselves dispute the Laurel,
I here renounce the Cause, and Quarrel.

FIDO.

FDELIIA

✿✿✿✿✿✿✿✿✿✿✿✿✿✿✿✿✿✿✿✿✿✿✿✿✿✿✿✿✿✿

FIDELIA *to Mr* URBAN.

From the fame *Magazine*

SIR, feveral Petitioners beg you'd procure

Of the *Britifh Meliffa* a true Pourtraiture,

For a fight of her Face (fhe has talk'd fo about it)

They'd rather give Money than languifh without it.

They hope the Expence will not prove very great;

However they'll freely fubfcribe for the Plate;

But yet for their Sakes who've their Hearts in their

keeping,

'Tis requefted the Nymph may be drawn when fhe's

fleeping.

For they fay, fhould her Eyes be unveil'd in the

Piece,

She might do as much Mifchief as *Helen* of *Greece.*

Now 'tis not for myfelf that I make this Requeft;

(I think Beauty a Trifle, a Toy at the beft)

But

But for the Petitioners, each my good Friend,

They knowing my Int'reſt with you, make me ſend.

So if for to get it you'll uſe your Endeavour,

Fidelia 'll acknowledge the Favour for ever.

P. S.

Sir, pray let the Artiſt you pitch on to do it,

Be warn'd of his Danger ('tis fit he ſhou'd know it)

And queſtion him whether his Valour's ſo good,

To venture to ſee her in warm Fleſh and Blood.

For tho' none upon Earth would oblige their Friends

    further,

I would not be guilty of any Man's murther.

FIDELIA.

✿✲✦✧✦✧✦✧✦✧✦✧✦✧✦✧✦✧✦✧✦✧✦✧✦✧✦✧✦✧✦✧✦✧✦✧✦✧

MELISSA *to* SYLVANUS URBAN.

From the *Magazine* for *October* 1735.

TO what *Fido* writes, I ſincerely Subſcribe,

    " A Houſe-wife's worth more, than the whole

        rhiming Tribe."

If

If *Fidelia*, or I, in our Station excell ;

Becomes not Ourselves, but our Neighbours, to tell,

 Your monthly Collections, I view with much Pleafure ;

Except your profound *Enigmatical* Treafure,

Your Riddles (excufe me !) I ne'er read, nor care for;

Tho' now I won't give you a *why* nor a *wherefore*.

Becaufe, I wou'd haften to tell you my mind ;

How great my Concern is, that *Fido*'s unkind :

I mean to *Fidelia* :—The cruel Deceiver !

In the Height of her *Doating* ;—thus bafely to leave
  her !

 How much fhe and I, were deceived in our Man !
  Sir,

Who cou'd have thought *Fido*, would prove a
  * *Drawcanfir* !

On

---

* The Name of a Hero in the *Rebearfal*

On both Sides, defend me! he deals out his Blows,

And falls to, moſt furious, on Friends, and on Foes.

Indeed for myſelf, I expected no Quarter;

But ne'er thonght poor *Fidy* ſhould thus catch a
    Tartar.

A *Soldier* of Honour is as ſure as a *Gun*;

And *ſrch* from his Colours would ſcorn for to run;

But he who deſerts, after all his high Boaſting,

Thro' his *ſhining Armour*, deſerves a Rib-roaſting.

While ſhe praiſes his *Conſtancy*,—'tis a ſad Caſe!

He vows, that his *Paſſion*, was all a Grimace.

And, we find in your *laſt*, (ſo piteous her fate!)

But the Turn of *two Leaves*, 'twixt her *Love*, and
    his *Hate.*

When *he* reads the *ſoft Lines*, which to *Sylvius*, ſhe
    * ſent,

If his Heart is not Adamant, ſure *he'll* relent!

Her *Warrior* forſake her!—May Honour forbid!

O *Fido!* O *Fido!* return to your *Fid!*

Poſt,

* *Gent Mag* Vol V. p 551.

POPE, OVID, and CHAUCER, have told us
    ftrange Things,

Of a monft'rous fine *Lady*, all cover'd with *Wings* ;

Her Feet on the *Earth*, and her Head in the *Skies*,

With thoufand of *Tongues*, and of *Ears*, and of *Eyes*.

She founds fuch a *Trumpet*, its *Notes*, they will
    tell ye,

Excell the *foft Airs*, of *ador'd* FARINELLI.

For her *Fav'rites*, a *Caftle* fhe has built in the *Air* ;

Wou'd *Fido* vouchfafe, but to ufher me, *there*!

The *Lady*, no doubt, has his *Name* on her *Lift* ;

Since he wields both a *Pen*, and a *Sword*, in his Fift.

For *he* who can *comment*, and *fight*, like a *Cæfar*,

Tho' *fhe* has fome Whimfeys;—muft certainly pleafe
    her.

To her *Caftle*, cou'd I have admittance; O then!

I'd hang up a *Tablet*, thefe *Lines*, and my *Pen*!

M m   Behold

Behold the *Pen*! which *Fido's* *Pen* engag'd,

When *Paper War*, he with *Meliſſa* wag'd,

Pacifick now, to native White reſtor'd,

A glorious *Trophy*, on this votive *Board*:

For faithful Service done, the grateful *Dame*

Devotes the *Pen*, which *Fido* laſh'd to *Fame*.

But, now, for *Fidelia's* Epiſtle profound,—

(Which ſhe hobbles about, like a *Lancaſhire Round*:)

That her *Vein* is moſt *eaſy*, by *Fido's* decreed;

But I'm greatly concern'd, now, I find ſhe can't

    read:

But to thoſe that can, I appeal for this *Truth*,

That I neither pretended to *Beauty*, or *Youth*.

Whoe'er will my Lines condeſcend to reviſe,

Will find I make free with my own *hollow Eyes*.

'Twas *Fido*, the Head of your *triple Alliance*,

Firſt ſent the *poor Things* (and my *Pen*) a defiance;

The innocent *Peepers*, he attack'd with much fpight,
Abandon'd Fidelia, wou'd veil them from *Light*.
Yet longs for to fee of my Face eveiy Feature;
Good *Urban*! convey my kind Thanks to the Crea-
    ture.
I hope fhe'll be fatisfy'd, when fhe is told,
Meliffa declares herfelf—*ugly* and *old*.
And furely the *Publick*, will grant this Confeffion,
From a *Woman's* own Hand, is an ample Conceffion'
But if *Fidy* perfifts,—I'll here lay before ye,
For her Confid'ration, a very fhort Story.

A *Monarch* more famous for *Wit*, than for *Grace*,
Once pluck't off a Mask, from a *Lady's* foul Face;
But finding her vext, that her Face had been fhewn,
He appeas'd her, by fhewing a *worfe* of his own.

My Meaning, as plain as a *Pikeftaff*, I ll make,
For I find dear *Fidelia* is apt to miftake.

      'T is

'Tis *rude* to expofe my poor Phiz to difgrace,
And thus, Like the *Monarch*, fhe'll fhew a *worfe* Face.

As *Fido* to *Sylvius*,—fo now, I declare,
If *Fidy* replies not;—here ends all the *War*.
Her *Champion* is gone;—and with *her*, I've done;
Who ftood out a *Blunderbufs*, fcorns a *Pot-gun*.

MELISSA.

PACIFICK STANZA's,

Addrefs'd to FIDELIA *and* MELISSA.

From the fame *Magazine*.

FIDY! ne'er heed a Slip in Play,
 Fate ha'nt the Game decided;
Tho' *one poor Knave* is trump'd away,
 Yet *Honours* are divided.

In

In Skill You like MELISSA fhine,
  Both prais'd by each Spectator;
Like gen'rous Gamefters Broils decline,
  Draw Stakes, and fhow good Nature.

PRIOR, with BOILEAU Strife to fhun,
  His humorous Vein expended.
As from a Pique their War begun,
  So, in a Jeft * it ended.

Like theirs, if your Contentions ceafe,
  How friendly Bards will greet ye!
Accept my offer'd Plan of Peace,
  Strike Hands, and fign a Treaty.

LUCIUS.

Anfwer

* See Epiftle to *Boileau*, in *Prior's* Poems.

Anſwer to the Stanza's *ſign'd* LUCIUS.

From the *Magazine* for *November* 1735.

AS LUCIUS now wou'd recommend,
  Of Honours, the Diviſion;
So URBAN once, *to both a Friend,*
Propos'd the *Bays' Partition.*

  Agree'd, agree'd ! MELISSA cry'd,
And to conclude the Quarrel,
  She ne'er pretended to divide,
But gave up all the *Laurel.*

  But FID, like mighty *Julius* burn'd,
Impatient of an Equal ,
  Demands imperiouſly return'd.
——Then let her take the Sequel.

Pleas'd

Pleas'd, she beheld a *Sharper* play

Her *Game*, with much Ill-manners ·

   To the smart *Knave*, tho' trump'd away,

She owes, *divided Honours*.

   The *Plan* accepted.—No Ill-will

I bear to Fid, or Fido;

   Tho' *both* on me have try'd their Skill,

Let *her* strike Hands.—as I do.

Melissa.

Fidelia's FAREWELL.

From the same *Magazine*

ALAS, Sylvanus ! I have been

   Almost devour'd with Grief and Spleen,

I may complain to you, a Friend,

My Sorrows, sure, will never End,

Not

Not SYLVIUS, nor the *Volunteer*,

Nor all the Complements I hear,

To eafe my Grief can ought avail,

Hard Cafe ! when fuch Encomiums fail.

But FIDO's gone ! too well you know it ;

I've loft a *Lover*, you a *Poet*.

Tho' yours is no fuch difmal Cafe,

You've Twenty to fupply his Place.

But poor FIDELIA has not One,

She's quite forlorn, now FIDO's gone.

I little Thought he was in Jeft,

So quite difcarded all the reft.

I hop'd his Word was to be taken;

Ah ! why no Law for Maids forfaken ?

Alas ! alas ! when I reflect

With what a conftant true Refpect,

He wrote of me three Months together,

My Patience runs I know not whither.

Three Months ! nay more ! he fent in *May* ;

Then, what fweet Words did FIDO fay !

He

He publifh'd it all *England* over,

That he was FIDY's Friend and Lover.

That fuch a Lover! fuch a Friend!

Shou'd in a Witch's Banquet end '—

Well—I've a thoufand Things invented

To make me ftay at Home contented;

Yet find, it is not to be done,

I muft crofs Seas, and turn a *Nun*:

To WINNEY's Convent I'll repair,

And fpend my Life in fomething rare.

Firft then, a Flag I mean to weave,

Which at my Death to him I'll leave,

(If all the World *that Man* can fhew,)

Who never was to love untrue.

Next I defign fome pretty Thing,

To add to th' Arms of *England*'s King,

When there fhall fuch a Prince be found,

As can pleafe all the Nation round.

But I forget—I've much to do,

And muft embark e'er this reach you:

N n   So

So pr'y—thee fay—that FIDY fends
A long Adieu to all her Friends.

FIDELIA.

❖❖'❖❖❖❖❖❖❖❖❖❖❖'❖❖❖'❖❖❖❖❖❖❖❖❖

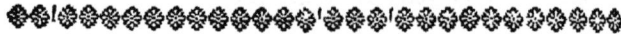

PASTORA *to* Captain FIDO *on his laft E-piftle.* p. 259.

From the fame *Magazine*

WILL FIDO then FIDELIA's Caufe refign'
  (Avert, ye Mufes, that unfair Defign')
The facred Stile of *Fido* ceafe to claim '
Obferve the Duty, or renounce the Name.

But not content to wrong that injur'd Fair,
'Gainft the whole Sex, you open War declare,
And fubtly urge, that *we* have no pretence
To raife our Faculties, and aim at Senfe ;
Gravely affirm, that all *we* ought to do,
Is to infpect a Family——and few.

Content

Content in Ignorance to drag our Chain,

And blindly ferve our haughty Tyrant Man,

Who, vainly fwell'd with his imperious Rule,

Thinks Nature deftin'd Woman a —tame Fool,

A meer Machine, devoid of Reafon's Guide,

And like the Brutes defign'd to footh his Pride.

    Your juft Preheminence *we* all allow,

But boaft afpiring Souls, as well as you ;

Indu'd with Reafon, active Pow'rs, and Will,

And can like you diftinguifh Good from Ill.

To us the tuneful *Nine*, with ready Care,

Whene'er invok'd, propitiously repair,

With gentleft Sentiments our Minds fupply ;

At their Approach all meaner Paffions fly.

Their chafte Delights are no Abufe of Time ;

Tho' you allege them as a monftrous Crime.

For why has Heav'n thefe various Gifts affign'd,

A fprightly Genius, or fagacious Mind,

If

If (as by your reftrictive Pen we 're taught)

The Application of them is a Fault?

Would you your juft Authority maintain,

And o'er our Minds a lafting Empire gain?

Good Senfe, alone, can teach us to obey,

And yield unforc'd Submiffion to your Sway.

Good Senfe---muft all our rebel Thoughts controul,

And root the Seeds of Duty in our Soul.

But if by barb'rons Laws we are confin'd,

Nor dare reform or cultivate our Mind,

Our upftart Paffions will affert their Force,

For nought but Reafon's Check can ftop their
      Courfe.

For if by Nature thefe fhould be fuppreft,

We're mere domeftick Drudges at the beft·

And fay—wou'd generous FIDO deign to rule

A haughty Termagant, or ftupid Fool?

Good Senfe, alone, muft rectify our Lives,

Make happy Husbands and---obedient Wives.

PASTORA.

    Captain

Captain FIDO's *Exclamation.*

HELP! help!—the Devil and all's a brew-
ing!

Defend me!—what have I been doing!

" All the *nine Mufes* on my Back '

Why fure the *Romps* won't make th' Attack ?

Yet hold—I'd rather have it faid

They're *on my Back*—than *in my Head*:

And they, I guefs, if throughly known,

Had rather be—upon *their own.*

For *Mufic is the Voice of Love.*

Hence the *cool Stream,* and *fhady Grove* :

And hence the *Latent* genial Fire,

That warms the Heart, and ftrings the Lyre.

Death to my Sight!—I fee 'em coming—

PASTORA * founds the Charge—with Drumming!

I yield!

* See the preceding.

I yield ! I yield ! to *Over-matches*,

And dread no Wounds like *Female—Scratches* !

FIDO.

Mrs MANAGE *to* Captain FIDO.

From the fame *Magazine*

What ! take a Woman to a Wife
Who leads a Wild, poetick Life ?

FIDO you 're right !—ne'er mind the *Flirts*,
But bid 'em mend their *Husbands'* Shirts,

Look to their *Family Affairs*,

And teach their *Children Pfalms* and *Pray'rs*,

Inftead of *Song* and *Roundelays*,

And idle Trumpery from *Plays.*

Flam me no Flams—of GRIERSON, BARBER,

And others, who fuch Fancies harbour :

I'm

I'm fure my *Husband* is no Fool,

And 'tis with him a ftanding Rule,

   " An Ounce of Prudence in a Wife

   " Is worth a Pound of Wit and—Strife."

For tell me if ye ever knew

A witty Wife that wa'n't a Shrew !—

At leaft, I'm fure, but very few.

Who's this, they cry that rails at Rhime,

And yet herfelf commits the Crime ?

—Ye Idiots ! have ye never feen,

A *Mimick* give a *Fop* the Spleen;

Play his own *Monkey Tricks* before him,

That to his *Senfe* he might reftore him ?

Befides—what's Rhime to *Poetry* !

Does *that* in jingling *Crambo* lye ?

At this rate *Sternhold*'s godly Metre

Is fweet as *Cibber*'s *Odes* and fweeter.

                            And

And many modern Sons of Fame,

Whom 'tis not fit for me to name,

Might pafs for *Poets*—tho' 'tis plain,

They never dar'd to be fo vain :

Nor had the *wicked Thoughts* at heart,

To foar above the Rhiming Art.

  Now if you like, good *Captain Fido*,

A Wife that *thinks* and *writes* as I do ;

I have a Daughter, Young and Fair,

Will fit your Pnrpofe to a Hair.

PRUDENCE MANAGE.

On the Unknown MELISSA.

From the fame *Magazine.*

TH' Unknown *Meliffa* may be Gay,
  And Blooming as the Month of *May* ;

Frefh

Fresh as *Aurora*'s Eastern Rays,

And wake a World to sing her Praise;

But Western Rays appear decay'd,

And Blossoms fall and Colours fade.

A Hint, *Melissa* ' if a Maid.

Or like *Apollo*'s Zenith Hour :

Or like a full blown Rose, her Pow'r,

Past Bud and balmy Honey Dew,

Unfolds, and sets her Seed in view,

Most sweetly deck'd in golden Hue.

Or like *Autumnal*, plenteous Horn,

With ripen'd Fruits, and Sheaves of Corn;

Indulgent to the Worlds she yields,

The Produce of her cultur'd Fields.

Or if the frigid Season's nigh,

Life's Winter, cold, benumb'd, and dry;

I value

I value not the outward Form,

The beauteous Soul is young and warm.

Then let *Meliſſa*'s Age be Morn,

Or Noon, or Eve, or Night forlorn;

Or let her outward Form be grac'd,

With ev'ry Beauty juſtly plac'd;

Or deck'd with ev'ry lying Sign,

That all within is not Divine.

Her Numbers, Humour, Force, and Fire,

My Soul enraptur'd, muſt admire.

W. C.

FIDO

✿✿✿✿✿✿✿✿✿✿✿✿✿✿✿✿✿✿✿✿✿✿✿✿✿✿✿

Fido *to Mrs* Prudence Manage.

From the *Magazine* for *December* 1735

MADAM,

Were I difpos'd to flatter,

I own you've giv'n me ample Matter.

—Flatter my felf—I mean—not you,

For Praife and Incenfe are your due.

Had I but half as much Pretence,—

Ev'n * Astrophil—that Foe to Senfe!

Shou'd in a *faithful Mirror* fee

The Fool—to whom he bows the Knee.

Forgive me, *Madam*, this Digreffion,

And liften to a *Rake's* Confeffion.

To fpeak the Truth, in modern Phrafe,

I've *feen the World*—and all its ways.

Convers'd

* Fido appears to have envy'd Astrophil and Sylvius on Account
of their Poems being adjudg'd to Prizes. Se *Mag for December* 1734, p 746

Convers'd with Male and Female Wits;

With *Lords—Knights—Country Squires—*and *Cits.*

Swept Stakes with *Dutcheſſes,* and—*Punks,*

And *honour'd* many a *jealous Hunks.*

With CLELIA I have paſt ſome Time,

For *Sonnet* famous, and *Sublime:*

And found the *good Poetick* Lady,

Tho' ſomewhat *Squeamiſh*—always *ready.*

Coquets I've known—but *Prudes!*—by Scores,

As pure as—*London* Common Shores.

Nay, ſo Impartial was my Love,

LAIS and I were *Hand and Glove:*

And once—heroically Tipſy—

I wiſely tilted for the *Gipſy.*

Religion was a ſtanding Jeſt,

Which ſerv'd to give the *Bowl* a *Zeſt.*

Green-porter—Op'ra—Maſquerade,

Love's *open Walks,* or ſecret *Shade;*

Tavern

Tavern—Affembly—Park—or Play,

Crown'd ev'ry Night—and ev'ry Day :

—In fhort—I've made a *fludious* Range

Quite from *St James*'s to th' *Exchange*.

To all which *Knowledge*, gain'd at Home—

I gain'd—*as much*—in *France* and *Rome*!

This is the *World* that I have feen,

Which gives Philofophers the Spleen :

Which gives your Men of Senfe Diftafte,

And will deceive us all at laft.

Young Rakes reform'd—good *Mrs Mannage*—

Are like an Heir—who, paft his Non-age,—

Comes early, to paternal Wealth,

In the ftrong *Flow* of active Health ;

'Ere *ebbing* Life his Schemes deftroy,

And leaves but Minutes to enjoy

Ev'n fuch was my propitious Fate !

Reflection didn't come too late .

Reafon

Reason affum'd her Pow'r in Time,
And made a Convert, in his Prime.

I never had—I thank my Stars !
A *dang'rous Wound* in *Venus'* Wars :
Nor did the *Flask's repeated Fire*
Make ALMA from her *Poft retire* ;
Firm and fecure the *Mud-walls* ftand,
Well lin'd within, well arm'd and mann'd :
I'm found as any Man alive,
And barely turn'd of—*thirty five*.

For twice feven Years I've ferv'd the Crown,
But if I marry—I'll lay down—
—" *Not fell*—(you'll fay)—there's no fuch Thing"
Then—*I'll excahnge*—God fave the King !
Retreat from all the Din of *War*,
And *Peace* and *Love* fhall be my Care.

Some

Some Acres of my own I boaſt—
Nor have I by the *Service* loſt ·
Which—and ſome Fortune with a Wife—
Will *keep the Rank* of middle Life.

This brings me, *Madam*, to *the Point*,
In which our Int'reſt is conjoint.
Yet ſome few Things we ſhou'd diſpatch,—
Preliminaries to the *Match.*

'Tis fit *your Daughter*'s Mind be known,
And that her Heart be quite her own.
No Pre-ingagement of her Love,
For that wou'd ruin all—*by Jove!*
My own Eſtate is free and clear,
And I'll have no Incumbrance *there.*

Nor will *you* treat the *Fair* with Force,
And truſt that Love may come of Courſe:

For

For tho' fhe leaves to you the Choice,

'Tis her's to give the cafting Voice;

She ought to fee and know *her Man*,

And then determine, as fhe can.

  I don't prefume to call in queftion,

By rafh Surmife, or ill Suggeftion,

Your *Daughter's* Merit—more than *yours*—

Your *Name*, and *Wifdom* both affures:

If fhe's the *Copy* of *her Mother*,

Te Gods! there's hardly fuch another.

  In Order, then, to clear the Way,

And hear what both Sides have to fay;

I'll wait—with leave of you—and *Spoufe*,

Upon *Mifs* MANAGE—at your Houfe.

FIDO

PARSON

✿✿✿✿✿✿✿✿✿✿✿✿✿✿✿✿✿✿✿✿✿✿✿✿✿✿✿

MELISSA, *in the Character of* PARSON LOVEMORE, *to Miſs* MANAGE.

From the *Magazine* for *January* 1736.

M Y dear PRUDENTIA!

I'm ſurpriz'd,

That your *Mamma* acts unadvis'd,

And meanly offers *ſuch* a Daughter

To FI, that Man of Blood and Slaughter !

Thus *Indians* (that he may be civil,)

Will make Peace-offerings to the Devil.

Awhile, I hop'd the martial *Scribe*,

Who hates the Female rhiming *Tribe*,

Would ne'er thy *Mother* like, nor *thee* ;

Since both can rhime as well as *he*.

Vain Hope, alas !——Of ſuch a *Rake*,

Who can a certain Judgment make ?

P p   His

His *Mind* is lighter, than his *Feather*,

And more unfix'd than *Wind*, or *Weather*.

——He now, I find, begins to treat;

And on Mifs MANAGE, fays he'll wait.

By this, the promis'd Vifit's made,

And thou haft feen the *killing Blade*,

With military Airs alert;

Grant Heav'n ' thou haft preferv'd thy Heart!

If he beheld thee with my Eyes,

His treach'rous Heart a Victim lies;

A Sacrifice for all the Wrong,

H' has done thy *Sex*, with *Pen*, and *Tongue*.

Tho' Wonders he can fpeak, and do;

Sure, PRUDY, he can't part us two!

Guefs how thy *Lovemore* is diftreft,

When jealous Fury ftings his Breaft.

Tho' I've *Difcourfes* ready pen'd,

In vain the *Roftrum* I afcend,

For thee, my Mind is fo perplext,
I lofe my *Notes*, and mifs my *Text*.

Not that I think thou'rt unfinceie ;
But 'tis thy Mother's Whims, I fear,
Who, as fhe now forgets her Name,
May grow regardlefs of her Fame.
She feems as fond of this fame FIDO,
As of the *Trojan* CHIEF was DIDO.
Should I in Silence then decline
The Anguifh of thy Heart, and mine ?
——Or muft I tell aloud to Fame
Our mutual Vows, my prior Claim ?
True to thy *Prieft* wil't thou abide,
Or be the faithlefs *Captain*'s Biide ?
Who tho' he may thy *Love* importune,
Yet his main Bufinefs is thy *Fortune*.

Canft thou his Courtfhip e'er receive,
Who proffers Love but to deceive ?

Who

Who venom'd Darts, at *Ladies* flyes,
And ftorms *the * Brothers of the Skies* ?
Ægeon thus *Olympus* fcal'd,
And heav'nly *Deities* affail'd.

CLELIA and FI, a Match fhould make,
A *Crack* would beft befit a *Rake.*
Their Principles would well agree,
He quits his Poft ;—her Virtue *fhe.*
And fince he found her always ready,
He cenfures each *poetick* Lady.
With as much Juftice, I might fay,
All *Officers* will run away,
Who the poetick Vein have found,
'Caufe FIDO could not ftand his Ground.

My Charmer, leave this Man of Lace,
And haften to my fond Embrace '
Be not feduc'd by his Brockade,
Embroid'ry, Ruffles, and Cockade;

For

* *Aftroph* and *Styteus*, who won the Aftronomy Prize, by their Poem

For fure my Garb more decent fhows,

My Gown, my Band, and hallow'd Rofe '

Thy Father will our Match approve,

Unknown to his meek *Tuı tle-dove* ,

Will join with us ın the Deceit,

Thy Mother's Projeϵt to defeat.

He knows full well what 'tıs we drive at,

Tho' for Peace' fake, he keeps it private.

To Wıles he often has Recourfe,

Sınce the grey Mare's the better Horfe.

H' has lately been my Houfe to vıew ,

And faid——'*twıll fuit my Daughter* Prue.

The more he fees thy Mother rapt in,

The more he hates, the bluft'ııng *Capt'm.*

Revenge thy *Sex* upon this *Heϵtor* '

At *W——n* meet thy faıthful *Reϵtoı*.

And when the *Goı dıan Knot* ıs ty'd,

To ————— I'll convey my Bride.

Then hafte, *my Fair*, and come away ;

My *Tythe* is better than his *Pay* ;

My *Houſe* is furniſh'd neat, and clean,

Fit for the Wife of any *Dean.*

And I've ſome *Acres* too, in Store

For you, and yours,   by

N. LOVEMORE.

FIDO's *Anſwer to the foregoing* Epiſtle *to* Miſs MANAGE, *ſign'd* N. LOVE-MORE.

From the *Magazine* for *February* 1736

YOUR common Sharpers of the Town
    Try forty Tricks to get a Crown ,

Put on the Porter, or the Peer,

Drink Hermitage, or Beer and Beer

So common Scriblers full of Arts,

In various Shapes diſplay their Parts ;

Write

Write Epigrams, or Panegyrics,
Heroic Strains, or dancing Lyrics;
And ftill—the better to beguile,
Change Names, as often as the Stile.

Thus the TWO BARDS—*profoundly* wife,
Who greatly dar'd the *nether Skies*,
Stript of their *dear poetick Fame*,
Laught at, and rally'd into Shame;
Their *little Talents* much too weak,
Now humbly play at *Hide and Seek*.

Who reads *bright* PARSON LOVEMORE o'er—
Finds a *new Name*—but *nothing* more.
Some wou'd fuggeft, that chafte FIDELIA,
Incens'd at fuch a *Wretch* as CLELIA,
And not well pleas'd with FIDO's Carriage,
Contriv'd this Plot to fpoil his Marriage—
—Set up the *Rev'rend Dotard's* Claim,
And wrote th' Epiftle in his Name.

—FIDELIA

—FIDELIA write it ?—Malice!—no---
She cou'dn't write, or act so low.

I grant indeed, that jealous Maids
Are apt to *swell* with—*teeming* Heads .
Yet still their Schemes have some Pretence
To Stratagem at least, and Sense.
But what a Stratagem was this!
(And how unlike to frighten *Miss*!)
—Fright her! with what? A *Man of Straw*!
As silly Birds are kept in awe.
She vows she does not know the Man,
Then let those point him out that can---
---Proclaim his *true Descent*---and whence
His *easy un-aspiring* Sense,
- Where SYL, or ASTRY, stands confest,
As much a *Poet*, as a *Priest*:
So PROTEUS—*grov'ling harmless* Ape,
Was known, and scorn'd in ev'ry Shape.

Think

Think ye I've nothing elſe to do
But write down Leſſons for *you Two*?
At firſt, indeed, in Condeſcenſion,
I gave ye wholſome Reprehenſion ,
But ſuch incorrigible Heads *!*
Like wild, unmanag'd reſty Steeds,
Defy the Bridle or the Spur,
To hold 'em in, or make 'em ſtir.

I give ye up! and will apply
To the *Truſtees* of Mr Guy ; *
His *Hoſpital's* the laſt Reſort
For Men of your *unhappy ſort* !
There, there I'll ſee you fixt for *Life,*
While I, *advent'rous,* take a Wife ;
And, if Miſs Manage proves a *Shrew,*
Untam'd by all *that I can do——*
As my *laſt Curſe*—I'll follow *you* !

Fido.
Parſon

Q q

* Founder of the Hoſpital for Incurables.

Parſon LOVEMORE *to* Captain FIDO.

From the *Magazine* for *March* 1736.

'TIS wicked,—I pronounce it, Sir,
 To inſult us, with the *Conjurer*!
The *Statute* is repeal'd, you know,
Therefore, your *Magic Skill* you ſhew ,
And conjure up to make a Farce on,
Two *Laymen* from one ſober *Parſon*;
And think, you, with Impunity,
May play the Dev'l with *them* and *me*!
— —But hold; you quite miſtake the Cauſe ,
For in the *Votes*, we find a *Clauſe*,
That's ſtill in force 'gainſt ſuch Offenders,
Who are no more than meer *Pretenders*.
Look to your Hits, ſagacious Captain,
Leſt this ſame *Clauſe* you ſhou'd be trap't in.

Your

Your *Fancy*'s no judicious Scout ;
But leads your Forces wildly out.
Truſt not again the treach'rous *Jade* ;
She'll drop you in, an Ambuſcade.

Well,—I'll convince you, if I can,
That you've, for once, miſtook your *Man.*
——No *Man of Straw*, I can aſſure ye,
Tho' I can't boaſt your *Force*, and *Fury.*
Your pretty *Flaſhes* I admire;
But keep due Diſtance from your *Fire.*
And ſo prevent the impious *Jeſt* ;
Th' attempt of *Blowing up* a *Prieſt.*
While I'm devoutly on my Haſſock,
No doubt, you curſe my *Gown* and *Caſſock* ;
Becauſe they pleaſe PRUDENTIA's Eye,
Much better than your glaring *Die.*
—*Play Hide and Seek*, you ſay—that's true ;
'Tis much the ſafeſt Game with *you.*

Q q 2　　　　　　—Howe'er,

—Howe'er, thefe *Truths* atteft I will ;
I neither Astry am, nor Syl.
Nor the much injur'd bright Fidelia ;
—I kifs the Book !—that I'm not Clelia.
And your dread Wrath, to keep a curb on,
I here declare, I'm not Syl. Urban.

Now what I am I'll next difcover ;
—Sir, I'm Prudentia's favour'd Lover ;
Had fome Acquaintance once with Fido,
And knew him fmitten by a Widow.
—It matters not or where, or when ;
—I had not taken *Orders* then—
But herded with the *Gay*, and *Vain* ;
—Nor had *he* made but one *Campaign.*
Some *Paftors* you may fee in *Town,*
In Publick walk without their *Gown* ;
To laick *Drefs* fo much they keep,
You'll fcarcely know 'em from their *Sheep.*

—Without

——Without my proper *Habit* on,

I'm feen by ne'er a Mother's Son.

True black my *Gown*, and eke my *Coat* is,

I vouch, *in Verbo Sacerdotis.*

A *Scarf* too, I've, at my Command,

But never rife, with *Plate* in Hand.

When the pil'd *Sweet-meats*, crown the Board,

I have my fhare——I thank my *Lord* !

And when the chearful *Meal* is o'er,

I drink the *Grace-cup*——feldom more,

Not *Beer and Beer*, but Wine and Water.

'——I ne'er difgrace my *Alma Mater.*

My grateful *Flock* confefs my Care,

And own they well inftructed are ;

They 're Orthodox, both one and all,

And never ftray to *Salters-Hall.*

——But where I preach, or where I dwell,

I'm not inclin'd, as yet, to tell.

True to my Honour and my Word,

As any *he* that wears a *Sword*,

PRUDENTIA, I will ne'er forfake,

Nor yield my Love to any Rake.

—But t'other Day, th' engaging Maid,

Thus to her faithful LOVEMORE faid,

" The *Wretch*, who has his Vows forgot,

" Be Shame and Infamy his Lot !

" Shun'd, nay abhor'd, by ev'ry Dame,

" Perifh his Memory and Name;

" May not one Friend, his Death bemoan,

" Nor grace with Epitaph his Stone!

—" And *fuch*, the Fate of *wretched* PRUE,

" If fhe proves falfe to Love and you !

" —This FIDO, ne'er my Heart fhall move ;

" The Rake abus'd FIDELIA's Love!

" His Prefence, like the Plague, I'll fhun ;

" —I'm in no hurry to turn *Nun*,

"—No

"——Nor to a *Convent* will retire,

" Unless my *Parson* should turn *Fryar.*

Now, Captain, what say you to *this?*

——Let's, by consent, appeal to *Miss.*

Let *Miss* to URBAN send her Vote,

Or for the Black, or Scarlet Coat.

What I propose, wou'd save, I think,

The sad Effusion of much *Ink.*

The wicked Waste of *Paper* too.———

——I'll *Miss* entreat, 'out more ado———

Now to declare the happy Man, Sir;

Then, let the unhappy take his Answer.

N. LOVEMORE.

F I N I S.